The Agatha Christie Centenary

On September 15th, 1890, Frederick and Clarissa Miller gave birth to a baby girl, Agatha Mary Clarissa, in Torquay, South Devon. A comparatively ordinary event, except for the immediate family. Yet over the next eight decades or so, Agatha was to make her name as the greatest writer of detective fiction in history, to the extent that on September 15th, 1990, Torquay will be the scene of great celebrations in honour of its most famous lady. Agatha Christie was one of the most prolific and certainly the most popular writers of fiction in the twentieth century.

Statistics of her phenomenal success abound – billions of copies of books sold, the many languages in which she was published, the record-breaking performances of her plays etc, but as a prelude to this publication, I would like to dwell on a few more human statistics. I wonder how many convalescenses have been enlivened by Agatha Christie books; how many trains or plane journeys have been made to pass more quickly; how many happy family evenings have been spent at her plays; how many television dinners have been consumed in wrapped engrossment trying to unravel one of her television mysteries; and how many people in foreign countries who have had their first taste of English life by reading one of her books.

It will be the purpose of this publication to examine a little more closely the person behind the legend, the reasons behind her success, and the prospects for the future. It is a fascinating story and at the same time a very human one. We will not hear its like again.

AGATHA

—1890

HarperPaperbacks
A Division of HarperCollinsPublishers
10 East 53rd Street, New York, N.Y. 10022

Editor: Lynn Underwood *Designer:* Terry Dean *Assistant:* Ewa Tabecka

Originally published for Agatha Christie Centenary Trust by Belgrave Publishing Ltd. *Directors:* John Nicholas, Mike Bokaie

Charles Osborne is the author of *"The Life and Crimes of Agatha Christie"* -Michael O'Mara Books
Janet Morgan is the author of *"Agatha Christie—A Biography"* -Fontana/Collins

First HarperPaperbacks printing: November 1990

Printed in the United States of America

HarperPaperbacks and colophon are trademarks of HarperCollins*Publishers*

CHRISTIE

1990 —

Little Agatha Miller

Little Agatha Miller.

"One of the luckiest things that can happen to you in life is to have a happy childhood. I had a very happy childhood. I had a home and a garden that I loved; a wise and patient Nanny; as a father and mother two people who loved each other dearly and made a success of their marriage and parenthood."

Frederick, Agatha's father.

Clara, Agatha's mother.

Agatha Christie started her autobiography, which she finished at the age of 75, with those words. References to her childhood are many, throughout the book, because it was the time she was truly happy and, to use her word, "safe." The house in which she spent that childhood, Ashfield, was her dearest memory. "Whenever I dream, I hardly ever dream of Greenway or Winterbrook [her houses later in life] it is always Ashfield . . ."

Agatha Miller was born into a comfortable but far from ordinary, middle class family in Torquay at the end of the nineteenth century. Her father, Frederick, an American was, in Agatha's words, "a very agreeable man" with an independent income. His days were spent at his various clubs and his evenings in entertaining, in the company of his wife. He was extremely gregarious, humorous and happy. His family, small wonder, adored him.

Agatha's mother, Clara, was quite a different personality. Agatha's own description of her mother, with whom she had a deep and close relationship, is fascinating because it is practically a description of Agatha herself, for they were so alike. "She was an enigmatic and arresting personality – more forceful than my father – startlingly original in her ideas, shy and miserably diffident about herself and, at bottom, I think with a natural melancholy."

It was from her mother that Agatha inherited her lively imagination, but it was also from her mother that she inherited a deep shyness and sense of insecurity.

Agatha was the youngest of three children. The oldest was Madge, most like her father, with her outgoing personality and love of "theatricals"; next was brother Monty who, from an early age, seems to have been a charming rogue. There was a ten year gap between Monty and Agatha, so Agatha's recollections of her childhood are almost like that of a beloved only child, since both her brother and sister were away at their respective schools most of the time.

The cornerstone of Agatha's early childhood was her wonderful Nursie "wise and patient", of unknown age (Agatha's father once guessed it at 64 since Nursie would not provide the necessary information), who provided stability and calm and counterbalanced

Agatha's mother, who entranced the child with quixotic and sometimes rather peculiar bedtime stories, such as the one about the poisoned candle which Agatha never forgot. Clara has been described by biographers as "psychic" – certainly she had a good intuition and seemed to possess the knack of being able to read people's minds on occasion – Agatha herself describes Clara as having "a naturally mystic turn of mind." She dabbled in religion and philosophies, and often changed her mind suddenly on family issues – such as the value of education for girls. She decided that Agatha should not learn to read until she was eight, but Agatha defeated that by teaching herself by the time she was five. Clara then decided that although her eldest daughter had had the benefit of a full formal education, Agatha would not. But Agatha had her books and the haphazard mixture of occasional music tutors and a small period, later, of part-time schooling seemed to have done her no harm – except perhaps it did nothing to improve her shyness.

Brother Monty.

In Agatha's own recollections there are few childhood friends – perhaps one or two who came to tea infrequently, and the children she met at the dancing classes she attended when she was very young. Circumstances probably made few children available (perhaps because their mothers, unlike Clara, believed in sending them off to proper schools) but, anyway, Agatha seemed to prefer her make-believe friends, her books, her dog, cat, canary and her wonderful garden which she transformed into fairy grottos and other magical places.

There were great "treats" in little Agatha Miller's life. Even after Nursie retired, much to the five-year-old Agatha's distress, there was always ample Jane, the cook, who cossetted the child with a continuous diet of scrumptious cakes and cream teas. Then there were visits to the two Grannies – Auntie-Grannie, who was Frederick's stepmother and Grannie B, who was Clara's mother. They were also sisters, the two Grannies, and usually to be found together at Auntie-Grannie's house in Ealing.

To Agatha these visits meant delving into Auntie-Grannie's store cupboard for handfuls of dates, french plums, raisins and cherries, to take out into the rose garden to savour. Both Grannies made frequent visits to the Army and Navy Stores and sometimes (another treat) Agatha went too.

The "safe but exciting" world of childhood came to an end when her father died, at the age of fifty-five, when Agatha was eleven. Her life was echoing that of her mother's – Clara's father had died at forty-eight, when Clara was nine and it had left her a solitary child in the care of relatives – just one more silken bond between mother and daughter. Clara was devastated by Frederick's death, she had loved him since she was ten years old, and she turned increasingly to the young Agatha for companionship.

Money was a problem too. Before Frederick had died he had begun to experience a decline in his family fortunes, mainly because of ill-judged investments. What little was left of the family money would later be swiftly despatched by Agatha's "charming rogue" of a brother, Monty.

Frederick had been the rock on which the Miller family was founded. Clara's restless energy and, often, morbid imagination were held in check as long as her beloved, amiable husband was there to bring her back to earth. With Frederick gone, Clara's restlessness surged up again. She began to travel, sometimes with Agatha, sometimes without, but it opened up a whole new world for the young girl and developed in her a love for travel which lasted throughout her life.

Madge with Jack on Matilda.

The situation in which they found themselves after Frederick's death increased Agatha's sense of insecurity. "We were no longer the Millers – a family. We were now two people living together, a middle-aged woman and an untried naive girl" said Agatha later in her autobiography. Sister Madge was married with a family of her own and brother Monty was in India with the Army.

Mother and youngest daughter were thrown together into an almost unbearably close relationship which imbued Agatha with such a strong sense of responsibility for her mother and the family home that later, when Clara died, Agatha's grief overwhelmed her.

But always, throughout her life, Agatha clung to the memories of those precious eleven years of childhood. In her conversations, in her autobiography, even in her books, memories of the halcyon days of Ashfield surfaced.

"Life seems to me to consist of three parts" she wrote later "the absorbing and usually enjoyable present which rushes on from minute to minute with fatal speed; the future, dim and uncertain, for which one can make any number of interesting plans, the wilder and more improbable the better, since – as nothing will turn out as you expect it to do – you might as well have the fun of planning it anyway; and thirdly, the past, the memories and realities that are the bedrock of one's present life, brought back suddenly by a scent, the shape of a hill, an old song – some triviality that makes one suddenly say 'I remember . . .' with a peculiar and quite unexplainable pleasure."

LYNN UNDERWOOD

Clara, Agatha's mother.

Agatha The Poet

Gold, Frankincense and Myrrh

Gold, frankincense and myrrh. …*As Mary stands*
Beside the Cross, those are the words that beat
Upon her brain, and make her clench her hands,
On Calvary, in noonday's burning heat.

Gold, frankincense and myrrh. *The Magi kneel*
By simple shepherds all agog with joy,
And Angels praising God who doth reveal,
His love for men in Christ, the new born Boy.

Where now the incense? Where the kingly gold?
For Jesus only bitter myrrh and woe.
No kingly figure hangs here – just a son
In pain and dying. …How shall Mary know
That with his sigh " 'Tis finished," all is told;
Then – in that moment – Christ's reign has begun?

That Agatha Christie was a lover of English poetry can be deduced from a quick glance at the titles of her murder mysteries, several of which are quotations from the English poets: *By The Pricking Of My Thumbs*, *Sad Cypress* and *Taken At The Flood* from Shakespeare; *The Mirror Crack'd From Side To Side* from Tennyson; *Endless Night* from Blake; *The Moving Finger* from Fitzgerald. But it is less generally known that she herself wrote poetry, and that she published two volumes of verse during her lifetime.

Agatha, in fact, began to write poems as a child. One of her earliest efforts, written at the age of eleven, begins:

"I know a little cowslip
and a pretty flower too,
Who wished she was a
bluebell and had
a robe of blue."

In her teens, she occasionally had poems published in magazines, and by the time she was in her mid-thirties and a successful writer of crime fiction, there were enough of them to be gathered into a slim volume which, in 1924, was published under the title of *The Road of Dreams*.

Agatha Christie's talent for poetry was genuine, but modest and of no startling originality. The finest poetry is made not from feelings but from words, and she was not sufficiently in love with words to become a poet of real distinc-

tion. She did, however, enjoy relieving her feelings in verse and, in doing so, quite often produced a pleasant little lyric poem.

The Road To Dreams is divided into four sections, the first of which, "*A Masque From Italy*", is a sequence of nine poems put into the mouths of such characters of the *commedia dell'arte* as Harlequin and Columbine, or Punchinello and Pulcinella. Written when Agatha was in her late teens, the Harlequin poems have a certain wistfulness which is appealing. They are of interest, too, in that they anticipate the Harlequin element which was later to creep into some of her short stories,

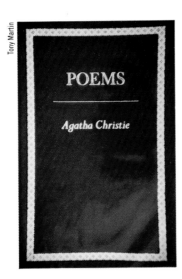

those involving that mysterious character Mr. Harley Quin.

Some of the poems in this early volume are romantically death-obsessed, and one of them, "*Down In the Wood*", which forty years later Agatha Christie still liked sufficiently to reprint in her autobiography, is rather good, with a last line that lingers in the memory: "And Fear – naked Fear – passes out of the wood"

Other poems deal with the passing of love, the horror of war, and the romance of the unknown. Again, there is a certain amount of evidence that the poet is "half in love with easeful death":

"Give me my hours within my Lover's arms! Vanished the doubts, the fears, the sweet alarms I lose myself within his quickening Breath –*And when he tires and leaves me – there is Death*."

Another of the poems, *In a Dispensary*, was written by Agatha in her mid-twenties when she was working in the hospital dispensary in Torquay. One of its stanzas clearly reveals the future crime writer's interest in the poisons on the dispensary shelves among which she worked:

From the Borgia's time
to the present day,
their power has been
proved and tried!
Monkshead blue, called
Aconite, and the deadly
Cyanide!
Here is sleep and solace
and soothing of pain
– courage and vigour new!
Here is menace and
sudden death! – in these
phials of green and blue!

It was not until 1973 that Agatha Christie, by then in her eighties, published a second volume of verse. Simply titled *Poems*, it reprinted most of the pieces from the earlier volume, and added several more which were presumably the only ones the author wishes to preserve from her poetic output between 1924 and 1973. They include descriptions of places she cared about, ranging from Dartmoor to Baghdad; some love poems, among them an affectionate sonnet addressed to her second husband, the archaeologist Max Mallowan; and one poem is oddly Betjemanesque in flavour, though hardly in achievement:

Afternoon tea by the
side of the road,
That is the meal
that I love,
Hundreds of cars rushing
past all the time,
Sunshine
and clouds up above!

Get out the chairs
and set up the tea,
Serviettes, too, are a must.
Never a moment that's
quiet or dull,
Sausage rolls
flavoured with dust! . . .

The most touching poem in the volume, and in the whole of Agatha Christie's poetic *oeuvre*, is "*Remembrance*", in which she envisages dying before her husband, which in due course she was to do. It ends with the lines:

I died – but not
my love for you.
That lives for aye
– though dumb,
remember this
If I should leave you
in the days to come.

She may not have been a lyric poet of great stature, but there is a certain quiet enjoyment to be derived from several of Agatha Christie's modest little poems.

CHARLES OSBORNE

Pre-War Society

House party at Cockington Court.

Photographs copied by John E. May

"I was now ready to 'come out' ... 'Coming out' was a thing of great importance in a girl's life. If you were well off, your mother gave a dance for you. You were supposed to go for a season to London... Of course, there could be nothing like that in my life. [Sister] Madge had had her coming out in New York and been to parties and dances there, but father had not been able to afford a London Season for her, and there was certainly no question of my having one now. But my mother was anxious that I should have what was considered a young girl's birthright, that is to say she should emerge like a butterfly from a chrysalis, from a schoolgirl to a young lady of the world, meeting other girls and plenty of young men and, to put it plainly, be given her chance of finding a suitable mate."

Cairo Races.

The time about which Agatha Christie (then Miller) was writing was 1906. She was just 17 years of age and had been in a succession of French 'finishing' schools for the previous two years, to prepare herself for genteel womanhood.

Her widowed mother, Clara, was ill – some gastro-intestinal upset which defied diagnosis and she also had a weak heart. Irritated by the ineptitude of doctors and concerned that she would not be able to afford to let Agatha 'come out' in London, Clara made a splendid decision which was the answer to both their needs – she and her daughter would spend the winter in Cairo.

Edwardian Society had several fashionable winter watering holes. Some, like Egypt and India, had evolved because of the presence of the British Army. In Victorian times, mothers with marriageable daughters found it expedient to congregate wherever there was an assured supply of young officers from good families. Agatha herself called it the "Popular Victorian Game". Although she was a very shy girl, she knew what Society expected of young ladies and therefore approached the task without trepidation.

"Cairo, from the point of view of a girl, was a dream of a delight. We spent three months there, and I went to five dances every week. They were given in each of the big hotels in turn. There were three or four regiments stationed at Cairo; there was polo every day; and at the cost of living of a moderately expensive hotel all this was at your disposal."

The rules of Society were still very Victorian. Young girls were chaperoned – young men were chivalrous. Agatha recalled that the rules decreed that a girl could not dance more than two of the dances on her programme with the same young man. Balls started late and went on until dawn, when one took breakfast en masse. Young ladies slept late and then spent the afternoons either having tea with female friends, playing croquet or tennis with males and females, or gathering at some equestrian event such as the races or polo.

In Cairo, going to the races was an essential part of the season and attended by the cream of British Society in residence. A photo in Agatha's own album shows a race meeting at which the Duke of Connaught and Lord Fielding were present. However, high society with marriageable offspring would, of course, be in London for the winter.

Agatha, who, in later life, would be totally absorbed by the ancient wonders of the Middle East, at the age of 17 declined any sightseeing trips preferred by her mother on the grounds that she had far too much to do. *"There's the fancy dress on Monday and I promised to go to the picnic to Sakkara on Tuesday..."* There were the obligatory pro-

Nellie, Aunty, Aggie, Noonie, Rex on roller skates on Torquay Pier.

Photographs copied by John E. May

posals of marriage, of course, but even 17 year old Agatha sagely knew that they were not to be taken seriously.

Back in Torquay, life was something of an anticlimax for a while. Torquay society was very sluggish, with few dances or other entertainments. The Millers knew very few people in London, although contacts made in Cairo resulted in a few invitations to dances in the capital city. The rescue came in the form of that quintissential Edwardian tradition – the house party.

Those with large, well-staffed houses in the country, usually invited friends to stay for the weekend or even a week in order to participate in some English traditional sport such as hunting, shooting, fishing or racing. It was essential for any lady to ride, which Agatha did – sidesaddle, as all ladies did then – and essential to have a supply of evening dresses, as everyone dressed for dinner. It was helpful to be able to play bridge and to be able to feign enthusiasm for the sporting activities of the menfolk, although it often meant standing in the freezing cold for hours on end.

Goodwood Races was a universally popular excuse for a house party but racing was not a pastime Agatha particularly enjoyed.

"It was an entirely racing crowd staying there, and racing language and terms were incomprehensible to me. To me racing meant standing about for hours wearing an unmanageable flowery hat, pulling on six hat pins with every gust of wind, wearing tight patent-leather shoes with high heels, in which my feet and ankles swelled horribly in the heat of the day. At intervals I had to pretend enormous enthusiasm as everyone shouted 'they're off!' and stand on tiptoe to look at the quadrupeds already out of sight."

Agatha was on a very limited income but, fortunately, the etiquette of the period protected her from any untoward expenditure. The hostesses of these house parties knew that the young girls they invited 'to make up the numbers' were rather strapped for cash

and therefore it was an unwritten rule that no other guest should attempt to encourage the young ladies to bet on either horses or cards.

Foreign travel was inexpensive before the First World War and so, when Agatha was invited to spend some time in Florence with a close family friend, she was happily able to go.

The Pre-War set of young people had new and thrilling experiences added to their usual round of socialising. The appearance of the motor car, for example. It opened up a new world of motoring weekends, with the thrill of travelling at twenty five miles an hour in an open car. Unfortunately, it meant the added expense of a new wardrobe. In those days, every activity had its own special uniform. For ladies it meant warm tweeds, large hats with huge veils and scarves, and, more often than not, waterproofs.

Agatha, never one to avoid a new experience, actually went up in an aeroplane in 1911 – a risky business at the time – but it was just a brief pleasure ride at a County Fair.

Agatha and friends on a picnic.

Lunch at Goodwood.

Dancing classes – Agatha in the centre.

Many of the young men of Pre-War Society were in uniform. It was considered the best way for a young man to 'finish off' his education, by doing a spell as a junior officer in one of the Services. Of course, the Victorian rules still applied to the sons of gentlemen – the eldest inherited the title or estate, the second went into the Army and the third went into the Church. Few of the young men of Agatha's acquaintance intended to make the Services their career but, alas, they had no way of knowing that within a few years they would be recalled or feel it their duty to sign on again as Europe plunged into war.

"I don't remember in 1913 having any anticipation of war" Agatha wrote *"Naval officers occasionally shook their heads and murmured 'Der Tag' but we had been hearing that for years, and paid no attention. It served as a suitable basis for spy stories – it wasn't real. No nation could be so crazy as to fight another except on the N.W. frontier or some faraway spot."*

But real it was and the generation which, in the years leading up to the war, had danced 'til dawn and picnicked in the sun were to reap the bitter harvest of the next four years. Afterwards, those golden years of 1910 to 1914 would be remembered as if they were a dream. Society would never be the same again.

LYNN UNDERWOOD

Agatha Christie returned to dispensing during the Second World War.

Phials Of Green And Blue

Agatha Christie wrote the poem *In a Dispensary* as a reflection of her early training during World War I as an apothecary or dispenser. It was not something that she had always wanted to do – she just fell into it really. She had started as a nurse in the Voluntary Aid Detachment (VAD) of the Red Cross Hospital at Torquay. When the hospital opened a dispensary she was asked to serve in it. She showed aptitude and successfully completed the examination of the Society of Apothecaries in London.

A gatha had a meticulous brain – one which filed away useful pieces of information – and she was capable of great concentration. Perhaps the *frisson* of danger that dealing with poisons brought to her life was what sparked off the idea for her first detective novel, but more of that later. Her own awareness of the dangers (here was a woman with a fertile imagination and a very strong sense of responsibility) is reflected in one of her own anecdotes from her autobiography . . .

During the course of my pharmaceutical instruction on Sunday afternoons, I was faced with a problem. It was incumbent upon the entrants to the examination to deal with both the ordinary system and the metric system of measurements. My pharmacist gave me practice in making up prescriptions to the metric formula. Neither doctors nor chemists like the metrical system in operation. One of our doctors at the hospital never learned what 'containing 0.1' really meant, and would say, 'Now let me see, is that solution one in a hundred or one in a thousand?' The great danger of the metric system is that if you go wrong you go ten times wrong.

On this particular afternoon I was having instruction in the making of suppositories, things which were not much used in the hospital, but which I was supposed to know how to make for the exam. They are tricky things, mainly owing to the melting point of cocoa butter, which is their base. If you get it too hot it won't set; if you don't get it hot enough it comes out of the moulds the wrong shape. In this case Mr. P. the pharmacist was giving me a personal demonstration, and showed me the exact procedure with the cocoa butter, then added one metrically calculated drug. He showed me how to turn the suppositories out at the right moment, then told me to put them into a box and label them professionally as so-and-so 'one in a hundred'. He went away then to attend to his other duties, but I was worried, because I was convinced that what had gone into these suppositories was 10% and made a dose of one in ten each, not one in a hundred. I went over his calculations and they were wrong. In using the metric system he had got his dot in the wrong place. But what was a young student to do? I was the merest novice, he was the best known pharmacist in town. I couldn't say to him 'Mr. P. you have made a mistake'. Mr. P. the pharmacist was the sort of person who does not make a mistake, especially in front of a student. At this moment, re-passing me, he said 'You can put those into stock; we do need them sometimes'. Worse and worse. I couldn't let those suppositories go into stock. It was quite a dangerous drug that was being used. You can stand far more of a dangerous drug if it is being given through the rectum, but all the same . . . I didn't like it, and what was I to do about it? . . .

There was only one thing for it. Before the suppositories cooled, I tripped, lost my footing, upset the board on

Copied by John E. May

which they were reposing and trod on them firmly.

Agatha's ingenuity saved the day! The same Mr. P. whom Agatha describes in this story, later showed his impressionable young student a dark-coloured lump of material and explained to her that it was curare – a fatal poison once it enters into the bloodstream. This insignificant little pharmacist from Torquay also explained to her that he carried it around in his pocket because it made him feel powerful. Agatha looked at him with renewed but somewhat disturbed interest. The memory of that occasion lingered with her for nearly fifty years and she used Mr. P.'s character in her book *The Pale Horse*. The characters in one of her earliest books *The Murder of Roger Ackroyd* discuss the merits of curare as an untraceable poison. In fact curare was mentioned in several other novels, but never actually used as the means of murder.

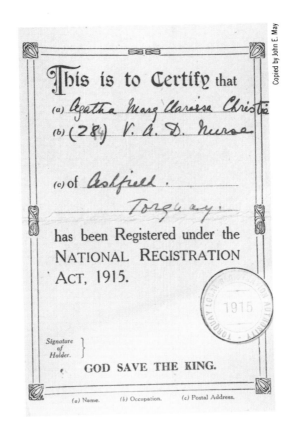

Meanwhile, back to Agatha's first book *The Mysterious Affair At Styles*. Some time before Agatha had started work in the dispensary, her sister Madge had challenged her to write a detective story. Now she was no longer rushed off her feet as a nurse, but sitting in the dispensary with much time on her hands between dispensing duties, Agatha decided to take up the challenge. Naturally, being surrounded by poisons, she decided to use one of them as the method of murder in her book. The story was littered with health professionals – the murder victim's doctor, Dr. Wilkins; 'One of the greatest living experts on poisons' Dr. Bauerstein; a young chemist's assistant, Albert Mace; and a VAD dispenser at a Red Cross Hospital (like Agatha herself) Cynthia Murdock. The poison used was strychnine, contained within a tonic for the heart, as was common practice during the early part of the 20th century. The descriptions of the poison, its uses and properties, are so detailed within the book, that it earned the novice crime writer an unheard of review – by *The Pharmaceutical Journal*. The reviewer wrote that "this novel has the rare merit of being correctly written – so well done, in fact, we are tempted to believe either the author had pharmaceutical training or had called in a capable pharmacist to help in the technical part."

It was the beginning, for Agatha, of a lifelong fascination with pharmacology, although she never practised as a pharmacist except once again during a time of national emergency in World War Two. However, she kept up her level of knowledge. One of her preserved notebooks, in which she jotted down all manner of useful facts, figures and notes to herself, is entirely devoted to toxic substances. A typical extract from Notebook 52 – **Poisons – possibilities for books**, reads:

Pentanol(Amyl Alcohol)C_3H_1,OH
Ethylene Glycol CH_2OH – colourless, sweet taste.
Substitute for glycerine – freeze and preserving substance. 100 grams drunk in Schnapps was fatal.

Look up Veronal, Pharodorm, Curral, Somnifen, Noctal, Phenoton, Nirvinal – (barbiturate derivation)

Kava-kava – narcotic pepper – produces joyous sensation – drowsiness

Amongst Agatha Christie's sixty-six detective novels, forty-one involve poison in an actual or attempted murder or suicide. Of her one hundred and forty-eight short stories, twenty-four also involved the use of poison.

In fact, Agatha Christie's knowledge of poisons has led to her being a source of great interest in the pharmaceutical world. Since that first review in *The Pharmaceutical Journal* in 1923 there have been numerous articles and papers written by members of the pharmaceutical fraternity about the Queen of Crime, the most recent being an article by Peter R. Gwilt and John R. Gwilt entitled "Dame Agatha's Poisonous Pharmacopoeia" published in *The Pharmaceutical Journal* in 1978 and a paper entitled "Dame Agatha's Dispensary" presented by Eunice Bonow Bardell in 1982 to the American Institute of the History of Pharmacy.

'I can't say that I enjoyed dispensing as much as nursing.' Agatha wrote in her autobiography *'I think I had a real vocation for nursing, and would have been happy as a hospital nurse. Dispensing was interesting for a time, but became monotonous – I should never have cared to do it as a permanent job.'* But she went back to it in the Second World War when she remarked *'On the whole it was much simpler than it had been in my young days, there were so many pills, tablets, powders and things already prepared in bottles.'*

LYNN UNDERWOOD

Trap For The Unwary

From beneath the black velvet hanging that draped the window a hand protruded. . . . He wheeled round and looked straight into the terrified eyes of a maidservant. . . . "Oh, my Gord! You've killed 'er!"

This early short story of Agatha Christie's appeared in a short-lived magazine called "The Novel" in 1923 and it is relatively unknown. We present it here for its first international reading.

The shabby man in the fourth row of the pit leant forward and stared incredulously at the stage. His shifty eyes narrowed furtively.

"Nancy Taylor!" he muttered. "By the Lord, little Nancy Taylor!"

His glance dropped to the programme in his hand. One name was printed in slightly larger type than the rest.

"Olga Stormer! So that's what she

calls herself. Fancy yourself a star, don't you, my lady? And you must be making a pretty little pot of money, too. Quite forgotten your name was ever Nancy Taylor, I daresay. I wonder now – I wonder now what you'd say if Jake Levitt should remind you of the fact?"

The curtain fell on the close of the first act. Hearty applause filled the auditorium. Olga Stormer, the great emotional actress, whose name in a few short years had become a household word, was adding yet another triumph to her list of successes as "Cora," in *The Avenging Angel*.

Jake Levitt did not join in the clapping, but a slow, appreciative grin gradually distended his mouth. God! What luck! Just when he was on his beam-ends, too. She'd try to bluff it out,

he supposed, but she couldn't put it over on *him*. Properly worked, the thing was a gold-mine!

BLACKMAIL

On the following morning the first workings of Jake Levitt's gold-mine became apparent. In her drawing-room, with its red lacquer and black hangings, Olgar Stormer read and re-read a letter thoughtfully. Her pale face, with its exquisitely mobile features, was a little more set than usual, and every now and then the grey-green eyes under the level brows steadily envisaged the middle distance, as though she contemplated the threat behind rather than the actual words of the letter.

In that wonderful voice of hers which could throb with emotion or be as clear-cut as the click of a typewriter, Olga called: "Miss Jones!"

A neat young woman with spectacles, a shorthand pad and a pencil clasped in her hand, hastened from an adjoining room.

"Ring up Mr. Danahan, please, and ask him to come round, immediately."

Syd Danahan, Olga Stormer's manager, entered the room with the usual apprehension of the man whose life it is to deal with and overcome the vagaries of the artistic feminine. To coax, to soothe, to bully, one at a time or all together, such was his daily routine. To his relief, Olga appeared calm and composed, and merely flicked a note across the table to him.

"Read that."

The letter was scrawled in an illiterate hand, on cheap paper.

"Dear Madam (it ran),
I much appreciated your performance in *The Avenging Angel* last night. I fancy we have a mutual friend in Miss Nancy Taylor, late of Chicago. An article regarding her is to be published shortly. If you would care to discuss same, I could call upon you at any time convenient to yourself.
Yours respectfully,
JakeLevitt"

Danahan looked slightly bewildered.

"I don't quite get it. Who is this

Nancy Taylor?"

"A girl who would be better dead, Danny." There was bitterness in her voice and a weariness that revealed her thirty-four years. "A girl who was dead until this carrion crow brought her to life again."

"Oh! Then ..."

"Me, Danny. Just me."

"This means blackmail, of course?"

She nodded. "Of course, and by a man who knows the art thoroughly."

Danahan frowned, considering the matter. Olga, her cheek pillowed on a long, slender hand, watched him with unfathomable eyes.

"What about bluff? Deny everything. He can't be sure that he hasn't been misled by a chance resemblance."

Olga shook her head.

"Levitt makes his living by blackmailing women. He's sure enough."

"The police?" hinted Danahan doubtfully.

Her faint, derisive smile was answer enough. Beneath her self-control, though he did not guess it, was the impatience of the keen brain watching a slower brain laboriously cover the ground it had already traversed in a flash.

"You don't – er – think it might be wise for you to – er – say something yourself to Sir Richard? That would partly spike his guns."

The actress' engagement to Sir Richard Everard, M.P., had been announced a few weeks previously.

"I told Richard everything when he asked me to marry him."

"My word, that was clever of you!" said Danahan admiringly.

Olga smiled a little.

"It wasn't cleverness, Danny dear. You wouldn't understand. All the same, if this man Levitt does what he threatens, my number is up, and incidentally Richard's Parliamentary career goes smash, too. No, as far as I can see, there are only two things to do."

"Well?"

"To pay – and that of course is endless! Or to disappear, start again."

The weariness was again very apparent in her voice.

"It isn't even as though I'd done anything I regretted. I was a half-starved little gutter waif, Danny, striving to keep straight. I shot a man, a beast of a man who deserved to be shot. The circumstances under which I killed him were such that no jury on earth would have convicted me. I know that now, but at the time I was only a frightened kid – and – I ran."

Danahan nodded.

"I suppose," he said doubtfully, "there's nothing against this man Levitt we could get hold of?"

Olga shook her head.

"Very unlikely. He's too much of a coward to go in for evil-doing." The sound of her own words seemed to strike her. "A coward! I wonder if we couldn't work on that in some way."

"If Sir Richard were to see him and frighten him," suggested Danahan.

"Richard is too fine an instrument. You can't handle that sort of man with gloves on."

"Well, let me see him."

"Forgive me, Danny, but I don't think you're subtle enough. Something between gloves and bare fists is needed. Let us say mittens! That means a woman! Yes, I rather fancy a woman might do the trick. A woman with a certain amount of *finesse*, but who knows the baser side of life from bitter experience. Olga Stormer, for instance! Don't talk to me, I've got a plan coming."

She leant forward, burying her face in her hands. She lifted it suddenly.

"What's the name of that girl who wants to understudy me? Margaret Ryan, isn't it? The girl with the hair like mine?"

"Her hair's all right," admitted Danahan grudgingly, his eyes resting on the bronze-gold coil surrounding Olga's head. "It's just like yours, as you say. But she's no good any other way. I was going to sack her next week."

"If all goes well, you'll probably have to let her understudy 'Cora,'" She smothered his protests with a wave of her hand. "Danny, answer me one question honestly. Do you think I can act? Really *act*, I mean. Or am I just an attractive woman who trails round in pretty dresses?"

"Act? My God! Olga, there's been nobody like you since Duse!"

"Then if Levitt is really a coward, as I suspect, the thing will come off. No, I'm not going to tell you about it. I want you to get hold of the Ryan girl. Tell her I'm interested in her and want her to dine here tomorrow night. She'll come fast enough."

"I should say she would!"

"The other thing I want is some good strong knock-out drops, something that will put anyone out of action for an hour or two, but leave them none the worse the next day."

Danahan grinned.

"I can't guarantee our friend won't have a headache, but there will be no permanent damage done."

"Good! Run away now, Danny, and leave the rest to me." She raised her voice: "Miss Jones!"

The spectacled young woman appeared with her usual alacrity.

"Take down this, please."

Walking slowly up and down, Olga dictated the day's correspondence. But one answer she wrote with her own hand.

Jake Levitt, in his dingy room, grinned as he tore open the expected envelope.

"Dear Sir (it ran)
I cannot recall the lady of whom you speak, but I meet so many people that my memory is necessarily uncertain. I am always pleased to help any fellow actress, and shall be at home if you will call this evening at nine o'clock.
Yours faithfully,
Olga Stormer"

Levitt nodded appreciatively. Clever note! She admitted nothing. Nevertheless she was willing to treat. The gold-mine was developing.

THE SPIDER AND THE FLY

At nine o'clock precisely Levitt stood outside the door of the actress' flat and pressed the bell. No-one answered the summons, and he was about to press it again when he realised that the door was not latched. He pushed the door open and entered the hall. To his right was an open door leading into a brilliantly lighted room, a room decorated in scarlet and black. Levitt walked in. On the table under the lamp lay a sheet of paper on which were written the words: "Please wait until I return. – O. Stormer."

Levitt sat down and waited. In spite of himself a feeling of uneasiness was stealing over him. The flat was so very quiet. There was something eerie about the silence.

Nothing wrong, of course, how could there be? But the room was so

deadly quiet; and yet, quiet as it was, he had the preposterous, uncomfortable notion that he wasn't alone in it. Absurd! He wiped the perspiration from his brow. And still the impression grew stronger. He wasn't alone! With a muttered oath he sprang up and began to pace up and down. In a minute the woman would return and then –

He stopped dead with a muffled cry. From beneath the black velvet hangings that draped the window a hand protruded! He stooped and touched it. Cold – horribly cold – a dead hand

With a cry he flung back the curtains. A woman was lying there, one arm flung wide, the other doubled under her as she lay face downwards, her golden-bronze hair lying in dishevelled

masses on her neck.

Olga Stormer! Tremblingly his fingers sought the icy coldness of that wrist and felt for the pulse. As he thought, there was none. She was dead. She had escaped him, then, by taking the simplest way out.

Suddenly his eyes were arrested by two ends of red cord finishing in fantastic tassels, and half hidden by the masses of her hair. He touched them gingerly; the head sagged as he did so, and he caught a glimpse of a horrible purple face. He sprang back with a cry, his head whirling. There was something here he did not understand. His brief glimpse of the face, disfigured as it was, had shown him one thing. This was murder, not suicide. The woman had been strangled and – she was not Olga Stormer!

Ah! What was that? A sound behind him. He wheeled round and looked straight into the terrified eyes of a maidservant crouching against the wall. Her face was as white as the cap and apron she wore, but he did not understand the fascinated horror in her eyes until her half-breathed words enlightened him to the peril in which he stood.

"Oh, my Gord! You've killed 'er!"

Even then he did not quite realise. He replied:

"No, no, she was dead when I found her."

"I saw yer do it! You pulled the cord and strangled her. I 'eard the gurgling cry she give."

The sweat broke out upon his brow in earnest. His mind went rapidly over his actions of the previous few minutes. She must have come in just as he had the two ends of cord in his hands; she had seen the sagging head and had taken his own cry as coming from the victim. He stared at her helplessly. There was no doubting what he saw in her face – terror and stupidity. She would tell the police she had seen the crime committed, and no cross-examination would shake her, he was sure of that. She would swear away his life with the unshakable conviction that she was speaking the truth.

What a horrible, unforeseen chain of circumstances! Stop, was it unforeseen? Was there some devilry here? On an impulse he said, eyeing her narrowly: "That's not your mistress, you know."

Her answer, given mechanically, threw a light upon the situation.

"No, it's 'er actress friend – if you can call 'em friends, seeing that they fought like cat and dog. They were at it tonight, 'ammer and tongs."

A trap! He saw it now.

"Where's your mistress?"

"Went out ten minutes ago."

A trap! And he had walked into it like a lamb. A clever devil, this Olga Stormer; she had rid herself of a rival, and he was to suffer for the deed. Murder! My God, they hung a man for murder! And he was innocent – innocent!

A stealthy rustle recalled him. The little maid was sidling towards the door. Her wits were beginning to work again. Her eyes wavered to the telephone, then back to the door. At all costs he must silence her. It was the only way. As well hang for a real crime as a fictitious one. She had no weapon, neither had he. But he had his hands! Then his heart gave a leap. On the table beside her, almost under her hand, lay a small, jewelled revolver. If he could reach it first –

Instinct or his eyes warned her. She caught it up as he sprang and held it

pointed at his breast. Awkwardly as she held it, her finger was on the trigger, and she could hardly miss him at that distance. He stopped dead. A revolver belonging to a woman like Olga Stormer would be pretty sure to be loaded.

But there was one thing, she was no longer directly between him and the door. So long as he did not attack her, she might not have the nerve to shoot. Anyway, he must risk it. Zig-zagging, he ran for the door, through the hall and out through the outer door, banging it behind him. He heard her voice, faint and shaky, calling, "Police, Murder!" She'd have to call louder than that before anyone was likely to hear her. He'd got a start, anyway. Down the stairs he went, running down the open street, then slacking to a walk as a stray pedestrian turned the corner. He had his plan cut and dried. To Gravesend as quickly as possible. A boat was sailing from there that night for the remoter parts of the world. He knew the captain, a man who, for a consideration, would ask no questions. Once on board and out to sea he would be safe.

THE MITTENS WON!

At eleven o'clock Danahan's telephone rang. Olga's voice spoke.

"Prepare a contract for Miss Ryan, will you? She's to understudy 'Cora.' It's absolutely no use arguing. I owe her something after all the things I did to her tonight! What? Yes, I think I'm out of my troubles. By the way, if she tells you tomorrow that I'm an ardent spiritualist and put her into a trance tonight, don't show open incredulity. How? Knock-out drops in the coffee, followed by scientific passes! After that I painted her face with purple grease paint and put a torniquet on her left arm! Mystified? Well, you must stay mystified until tomorrow. I haven't time to explain now. I must get out of the cap and apron before my faithful Maud returns from the pictures. There was a 'beautiful drama' on tonight, she told me. But she missed the best drama of all. I played my best part tonight, Danny. The mittens won! Jake Levitt is a coward all right, and oh, Danny, Danny – I'm an actress!"

AGATHA CHRISTIE

Michael Parkinson's Confession Album – 1973
(Sidgwick & Jackson)

In 1972, television personality Michael Parkinson began to compile a book called "Michael Parkinson's Confession Album" in which famous people responded to a questionnaire about their likes and dislikes. Dame Agatha Christie Mallowan duly filled in her "confession" form and made this comment to Michael Parkinson in an accompanying letter:

"Filling up your confessional brought back to me very strong memories of my early Victorian youth. I well remember all our family and friends filling up various confessional albums belonging to my grandmother, great aunt and so on. Everyone enjoyed it immensely."

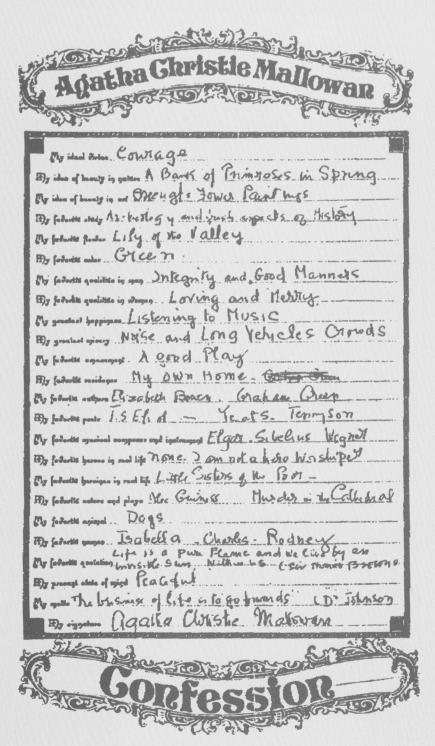

A Whirlwind Courtship

THE MYSTERIOUS AFFAIR AT STYLES

By AGATHA CHRISTIE

Agatha Christie

When Agatha Miller met Archie Christie in 1912, she was not quite twenty-two, he was nearly twenty-three. There is a sketch in one of the novels Agatha wrote as Mary Westmacott, *Unfinished Portrait*, in which the heroine dances with a dashing young man at a regimental ball. He comes, she says, 'in a whirlwind' into her life, spirits her away from her fiancé and changes everything. That was what happened to Agatha.

She had made a couple of false starts. There had been an understanding with Wilfrid Pirie, a sub-lieutenant in the Navy, whose mother Agatha admired, and then there was Reggie Lucy. His sisters played tennis and croquet with Agatha at home in Torquay. Cheery and informal, he had asked her to bear him in mind, if no one else turned up. When Archie appeared, that was that.

They first saw each other at a dance given by Lord and Lady Clifford of Chudleigh, who had invited some of the garrison at Exeter. Shortly afterwards, Archie happened (or so he said) to be passing Agatha's mother's house, Ashfield, on his motorbike; what was more natural than that he should drop in? He was tall, well-built, with fair, crisply curling hair, cut short. His nose had a small crinkle, his eyes were blue and he was very determined. Three months before he met Agatha he had applied to

And Marriage

Archie Christie by
Lafayette 1918.

join the Royal Flying Corps, as a qualified aviator, still a novel and risky profession, and as soon as he was accepted he asked Agatha to marry him. 'I want to dreadfully', Agatha told her mother but Mrs. Miller insisted that they wait, for Agatha had only £100 a year from her grandfather's trust and Archie his subaltern's pay. Then, in the summer of 1914, war came.

Archie was sent to France and Agatha worked in a hospital in Torquay. When he came home on leave at Christmas, he was gay and frivolous, hiding the fear and strain through which he was living. Agatha was anxious and earnest; for the last three months she had seen the dead and wounded coming home. The two young people quarrelled, made it up, talked of marrying, decided not to, changed their minds. On Christmas Eve 1914, they married by special licence; on Boxing Day Agatha saw Archie off again to France.

It was nearly four years before Agatha's married life really began. In the autumn of 1918, to her great joy, Archie was posted home to a job in the Air Ministry in London. He had fought a brave war – he had been mentioned in despatches four times and awarded the C.M.G. and D.S.O. — and was now a Colonel, at the age of twenty-nine. Both he and Agatha were older and wiser, for they had known tiredness and grief, suffering and death. Now everything seemed heavenly. When the war ended in November, Archie found a job in the City that brought in £500 a year. With this, his gratuity and Agatha's £100, they had enough, just, to rent, decorate and furnish a pretty flat in London, to employ a cook/housemaid and, in late 1919, a nurse. For in August their daughter Rosalind was born; Archie adored her. At weekends the family often returned to Ashfield, to see Mrs. Miller, picnic on the moors, walk by the sea and join Agatha's old friends for impromptu parties. Archie enjoyed these less than his wife.

His job was demanding and it was difficult to forget the war. He was edgy, his sinuses gave him trouble – and then, hours later, he would ask for treacle, sweet and viscous, to comfort his nervous stomach.

Calmly, unostentatiously, Agatha and Archie built their life together. He pressed on with his work in the City; she, to her surprise, found that she had a profession of her own. In 1919 John Lane, the publisher, had seen and liked *The Mysterious Affair at Styles*, a detective story Agatha had written during the war, to prove to her sister that she could do it. The book sold well and Agatha signed a contract to produce five more. By the end of 1921 *The Secret Adversary* was ready for publication and she was working on *Murder on the Links* and a series of stories for the *Sketch*. At this point, however, there was an interruption.

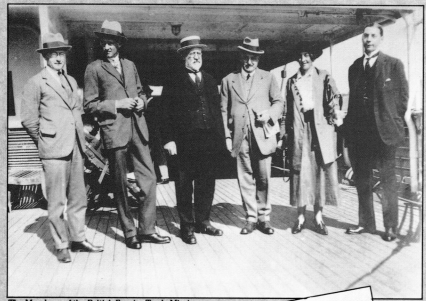

The Members of the British Empire Trade Mission.

CHRISTIE VISITS VERNON PACKERS

VERNON, Sept. 24.—Col. A. Christie of the British Empire Exhibition Mission spent Saturday in Vernon, when he visited the packing houses and canneries, as well as a number of the orchards in the Coldstream district, and in the evening addressed a meeting arranged by the Vernon Board of Trade in the City Club. Mayor Costerton presided. Col. Christie motored to Kelowna

Archie, Major Belcher, Agatha.

Encouraged by Agatha, Archie left his job and accepted an offer from one of his former schoolmasters, Major Belcher, who was a colourful blusterer, unimaginably inefficient, but none-the-less had a talent for persuading people to employ him in important administrative posts. Major Belcher had been assigned to drum up support for the British Empire Exhibition, to take place in London in 1924, and he proposed to do so by making a ten-month trip to Canada, Australia, New Zealand and South Africa. Archie was invited to come as Financial Adviser, expenses paid, for a fee of £1,000. If Agatha wished to accompany him, her travelling costs would be covered and her hotel bills could come out of Archie's fee. She longed to see the world and her mother had always told her that a wife's place was with her husband, so she left Rosalind with her sister, and took off.

The expedition was wearing but stimulating, for Agatha at least. Archie had to cope with Belcher's tantrums and when he came home he had to look for a job. There was a rough patch for several weeks and, once he found a post, he suspected that his employers were a bit shady. Archie was worried and depressed until, fortunately, an old friend offered him something more satisfactory. Agatha, meanwhile, was flourishing.

A day on the Zambezi for Agatha.

She had now published five books and acquired a literary agent. She bought a car and learnt to drive and she and Archie felt sufficiently secure financially to leave London and buy a property in Berkshire, near the golf course at Sunningdale. Golf, however, was the beginning of the end of the Christie marriage.

Sunningdale was comfortable, conventional and dull. Agatha had few friends there; the people she met were, she said, either smart and rich or interested only in gardens. Archie was less critical. He worked long hours during the week and on Saturdays and Sundays he liked to play golf and to talk about it over dinner. When at the end of 1924, Agatha declared that they must move, Archie persuaded her to stay in Sunningdale, in a bigger, grander house. They renamed it, *Styles*. Agatha bravely took out a subscription so that she could practise on the new Wentworth golf course; alas, she was neither very good nor very interested. Archie went away for a weekend with golfing friends in Surrey. There he met Nancy Neele, gregarious, sympathetic and as keen on golf as he was.

Nancy was uncomplicated, Agatha the opposite. Agatha was reserved, observant and imaginative, and concentrated increasingly on her own preoccupations. In 1926 her mother died and she spent days clearing Ashfield, sweeping away the memories with the

Agatha waiting for tea on the beach in Honolulu.

Archie Christie surfing in Honolulu.

cobwebs. She wanted comfort but Archie was impatient. He needed, he said, a peaceful home and a happy wife. At the beginning of August he confessed that he was in love with Nancy Neele. Agatha was devastated.

Archie moved to his club, Agatha tried to understand what had happened. Lonely, miserable and worn out, she could neither eat nor sleep. Early in December, suffering intolerably, she drove away from Styles in the middle of the night and disappeared. Ten days later she was found at an hotel in Harrogate. Doctors call this 'an hysterical fugue'; in her escape from Styles and all it meant. Agatha had forgotten who she was.

When she recovered, she agreed to let Archie go. They were divorced in 1928 and he married Miss Neele. Agatha went on with her writing and in 1930 she married Max Mallowan, the archaeologist. She did not see Archie again but, years later, when Nancy died, she wrote to him to say that, having found happiness in her marriage to Max, she could understand Archie's loss. Years after Agatha's own death, Archie's letters and flying certificate turned up in an old writing-case of Agatha's, with her first wedding ring – relics of a marriage that, like unseasoned wood, went out of shape when it stopped growing.

DR. JANET MORGAN

Rosalind

Agatha and Rosalind 1923.

'There is nothing more thrilling in this world', Agatha
Christie wrote in her *Autobiography*, *'than having a child
that is yours and yet is mysteriously a stranger . . . it is
like a strange plant which you have brought home,
planted, and can hardly wait to see how it will turn out'.*

While it delighted her to see her daughter growing up, she was conscious all the time that Rosalind had her own character and inclinations and that she would develop in her own way. In two of her detective stories, *Ordeal By Innocence* and *They Do It With Mirrors*, Agatha described the consequences of a woman's overwhelming possessive love. Her relationship with her own child was affectionate but not smothering. Each of them she believed, should have her independence.

Rosalind Margaret Clarissa was born on August 5th 1919 at Ashfield, Agatha's mother's house in Torquay. Archie Christie was devoted to his daughter; he and Agatha painted her nursery with a pale yellow wash, with an animal frieze round the top of the wall. Rosalind's first home was at the Chris-

ties' flat at Addison Mansions in London but she spent a good deal of time in Torquay and in her third year, while her parents were travelling on the Empire Tour, she and her nurse were parked at Abney, Agatha's sister's house in Cheshire.

When Rosalind was four, her parents moved to Scotswood in Sunningdale, where there was a garden for her, and a year later they bought Styles, with its lawn, wild garden and shallow stream. Here, too, Rosalind found a guide and friend, Charlotte "Carlo" Fisher, a young Scotswoman who had come as Agatha's secretary but who quickly took her daughter in hand. Rosalind was bright, beautiful, strong-minded and terrifyingly direct. Two out of three of her governesses had been hopeless, for they lacked imagination and authority. When the best of these left to take up a post

abroad, her successor could not cope. Rosalind had become rebellious and naughty. Carlo Fisher changed all this.

It was fortunate for Rosalind, as well as for Agatha, that Carlo was there to support them in the difficult days of 1926 and the unhappy year that followed. After her parents' divorce, Rosalind continued to see her father; she wrote to him regularly from Caledonia, her boarding school at Bexhill, and later from Benenden. Nor did she resent her stepfather, although his life of writing and reading, punctuated by good meals, struck her as pleasantly self-indulgent, until she accompanied Max and Agatha on an archeological expedition and saw how hard he worked.

Rosalind was then eighteen. She had been sent to stay *en pension* in Switzerland, France and Germany, to improve her languages, before a London season.

DR. JANET MORGAN

Photographs copied by John E. May

At the telephone.

With her daughter, Rosalind: Agatha Christie, the great detective-story writer.

At her writing table.　At work with her type-writer.

In her drawing-room: the author of the series of detective stories we begin this week.

With "Tutankhamen" cushions: Agatha Christie and her little girl.

CREATOR OF THE MOST INTERESTING DETECTIVE SINCE SHERLOCK HOLMES: AGATHA CHRISTIE.

Agatha and Rosalind 1925.

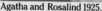

Rosalind aged 18.

She shared this with a friend, whose mother took the girls to parties and dances. (Fortunately for Agatha, who would have hated it.) This was followed by a trip to stay with friends in South Africa. Shortly after Rosalind returned, war broke out. She looked for work as a land girl and applied to join the Women's Auxiliary Air Force and the A.T.S. Before either could reply, Rosalind became engaged to Hubert Prichard, an officer in the Royal Welch Fusiliers, whose home was at Pwllywrach in Wales. They were married in 1940; in September 1943 their son Mathew was born. In 1944 Hubert was reported missing and in August Rosalind learnt that he had been killed. She stayed on at Pwllywrach, coping with a small baby, in an unheated house, with no staff and a yard of recalcitrant animals. Agatha spent considerable time with Rosalind and Mathew in Wales, helping to furnish the large house with some of her own furniture.

A gatha admired her daughter's courage and stamina. She was delighted when, in October 1949, Rosalind announced that she was marrying Anthony Hicks, an amusing, scholarly man, interested in gardens, cosmology, books, butterflies, all manner of people and things, and, like Agatha, passionately fond of travel.

After Rosalind and Anthony married the family spent every spring and summer at Agatha's house in Devon, visited her at Wallingford at other times, while Agatha, in her turn, stayed frequently at Pwllywrach. Agatha lived to become a great grandmother and she was delighted.

Agatha always regarded her family; in particular Rosalind, as the best critics of her work.

In 1968, the year after Mathew's marriage, Rosalind and Anthony moved to her mother's house, Greenway, in South Devon. They live there still. Rosalind keeps a close eye on the way in which Agatha Christie's work is treated, fending off those who would vulgarise or distort it. It would have been easy for her to have been overwhelmed by her mother's reputation and the demands of publishers, agents and producers; in death, if not in life, Agatha could have been a possessive parent. But Rosalind and Anthony have their house, a garden of splendid shrubs and trees, their own friends and interests. Wisely, neither Agatha nor Rosalind invaded each other's lives.

DR. JANET MORGAN

Hercule Poirot – Fiction's Greatest Detective

The character of Hercule Poirot was the character with whom Agatha Christie lived the longest. She created him for her first book, *The Mysterious Affair At Styles* (1920) and last wrote of him in *Hallowe'en Party* (1969), although several collections of Poirot short stories were reissued after that date. So, for nearly 50 years, Agatha had this strange relationship with her creation. She alternated between exasperation and admiration of Poirot. She removed him from several of the stories which she made into plays because his character was too dominating for the stage, she felt. But the public adored him. She had drawn a character that was so compelling that they could not get enough of him.

Here, in an article she herself wrote for The Daily Mail in January 1938, as a prelude to her serial thriller *Date With Death**, Agatha explains the brilliant little man and her own relationship with him.

*Issued in novel form as "Appointment With Death".

How did the character of Hercule Poirot first come into being? Difficult to say – and I realise that he made his appearance not at all in the manner he himself would have wished!

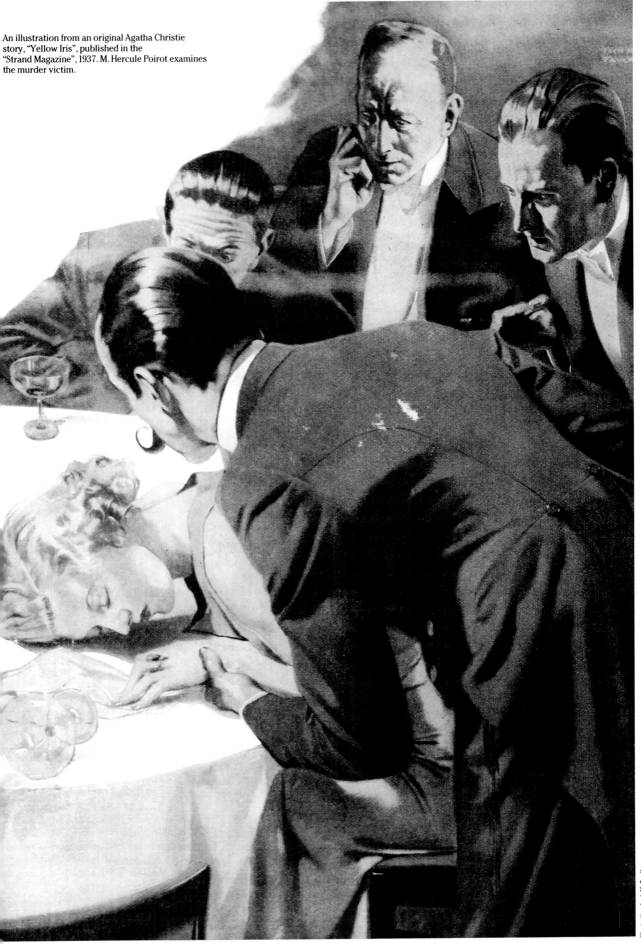

An illustration from an original Agatha Christie story, "Yellow Iris", published in the "Strand Magazine", 1937. M. Hercule Poirot examines the murder victim.

"Hercule Poirot first", he would have said, "and then a plot to display his remarkable talents to their best advantage". But it was not so. The plot of the story (*The Mysterious Affair At Styles*) was roughed out and then came the dilemma: A detective story – now, what kind of detective?

It was in the early autumn of 1914 – Belgian refugees were in most country places – why not have a Belgian refugee, a former shining light of the Belgian police force?

Handsome Moustache

What kind of a man should he be? A little man, perhaps, with a somewhat grandiloquent name. Hercule something? Hercule Poirot? Yes, that would do. He should be very neat – very orderly. (Is that because I am a wildly untidy person myself?)

Such was the first rough outline – mostly you will note, externals. But certain traits followed almost automatically. Like many small dandified men, he would be conceited and he would of course (why of course?) have a handsome moustache.

That was the beginning. Hercule Poirot emerged from the mists and took concrete shape and form.

There was more in the little man than I had ever suspected. There was, for instance, his intense interest in the psychology of every case.

As early as *The Murder On The Links* he was showing his appreciation of the mental processes of a murderer and insisting that every crime had a definite signature.

I Have Seen Him!

And now what of the relations between us – between the creator and the created? Well – let me confess it – there has been at times a coolness between us! There are moment when I have felt: "Why – why – why did I ever invent this detestable, bombastic, tiresome little creature?"

Eternally straightening things, eternally boasting, eternally twirling his moustache and tilting his egg-shaped head. Anyway, what is an egg-shaped head? When people say to me, "Which way up is the egg?" do I really know? I don't, because I never do see pictorial things clearly, but nevertheless I know that he has an egg-shaped head covered with suspiciously black hair, and I know his eyes occasionally shine with a green light, and twice in my life I have actually

seen him!

Once in a boat going to the Canary Islands, and once having lunch at the Savoy, I have said to myself: "Now, if you had only had the nerve, you could have 'snap-shotted' that man in the boat, and you could perhaps have gone to the man in the Savoy and explained matters". But life is full of lost opportunities.

Rebelled Bitterly

If you are doubly burdened, first by acute shyness, and secondly by only seeing the right thing to do or say twenty-four hours later, what can you do? Only write about quick-witted men and resourceful girls, whose reactions are like greased lightning.

Yes, there have been moments when I've disliked M. Hercule Poirot very much indeed, when I have rebelled bitterly against being yoked to him for life (usually at one of these moments that I receive a fan letter saying "I know you must love your little detective, by the way you write about him").

But now, I must confess it, Hercule Poirot has won. A reluctant affection has sprung up for him. He has become more human, less irritating.

In spite of his vanity he often chooses deliberately to stand aside and let the main drama develop. He says, in effect, "It is their story – let them show you why and how this happened." (He knows, of course, that the star part is going to be his all right later. He may make his appearance at the very end of the first act, but he will take the centre of the stage in the second act, and his big scene at the end of the third act is a mathematical certainty.)

At His Best

He has his favourite cases. In *The Murder of Roger Ackroyd* he was at his best investigating a crime in a quiet country

village and using his knowledge of human nature to get at the truth.

In *The Mystery of the Blue Train* I have always suspected he was not at his best, but the solving of *Lord Edgeware Dies* was, I consider, a good piece of work on his part, though he gives some of the credit to Hastings.

Three-Act Tragedy he regards as one of his failures, though most people do not agree with him. His final, remark at the end of that case has amused many people. Remember how he said "It might have been me" when Mr. Satterthwaite declared that anyone might have drunk the poisoned cocktail?

Hercule Poirot cannot see why this should be thought so amusing. He considers that he merely stated an obvious truth. Of all his cases *Cards on the Table* was the murder which won his complete technical approval. *The Death on the Nile* saddened him, since he saw so much of the drama preceding the crime.

Since *A Date With Death* my new book, which begins in The Daily Mail next Wednesday, is sub judice, he must not comment on it here. Let me only say that three points in it appealed to him strongly.

First, the fact that he undertook the case at the express desire of a man whose passion for the truth was equal to his own. Secondly, the technical difficulties of the investigation made a special appeal to him, the necessity of reaching the truth in 24 hours without the help of expert evidence of any kind.

And thirdly, he was fascinated by the peculiarly psychological interest of the case, and particularly by the strong malign personality of the dead woman.

Well, I have given you some of my impressions of Hercule Poirot. They are based on an acquaintance of many years' standing. We are friends and partners. I am beholden to him financially.

On the other hand he owes his very existence to me. In moments of irritation I point out that by a few strokes of the pen (or taps on the typewriter) I could destroy him utterly.

He replies grandiloquently: "Impossible to get rid of Hercule Poirot like that. He is much too clever!"

And so, as usual, the little man has the last word...

AGATHA CHRISTIE
Copyright Agatha Christie 1938

Illustration Jack M. Faulks.

Enter

Allen Lane And The Penguins

Agatha Christie's first book *The Mysterious Affair at Styles* featured the Belgian detective Hercule Poirot and this quixotic character was to prove so enduringly popular with her readers that Agatha had to revive him again and again. Anyway, he proved lucky for her in that he attracted The Bodley Head and from then on her career as a professional writer took off. This was the beginning of her relationship with John Lane and his nephew Allen...

Her relationship with John Lane was not always happy. Agatha felt that he took advantage of her ignorance in his business dealings with her. However, her relationship with John Lane's nephew Allen, who was to inherit the firm from his uncle after his death, was much closer.

Allen Lane later created a company called Penguin which conceived one of

the publishing industry's historic marketing exercises – the sixpenny paperback – which immediately brought literature to the masses, and Agatha Christie was one of the first authors to offer her work for the Penguin experiment, with dynamic results.

The partnership and friendship between Allen Lane and Agatha Christie was strong and successful. In a previously unpublished piece of work, Agatha herself describes almost half a century of mutual respect. **Agatha Christie writes:**

My friendship with Allen Lane came into being sometime between forty and fifty years ago.

My first connection with the publishing house of the Bodley Head was when I received a letter from John Lane suggesting that I should call on him to discuss a manuscript which I had sent to the Bodley Head about eighteen months previously and the existence of which I had entirely forgotten. It had already been refused by six other publishers without any words of encouragement – and I had quite given up hope of ever having a book published.

I shall always remember my first meeting with John Lane. I was paralysed with shyness as I went into his little office, with its chairs and its table crowded with manuscripts and drawings and oil paintings. He looked to me like an old-fashioned Sea Captain, with his small grey beard and shrewd twinkling blue eyes.

He said quite kindly:

"Sit down, my dear, sit down –" I looked round. There was nowhere to sit. "Ah! Yes," he said, and moved a couple of oil paintings, a book or two, and dusted off a chair.

"About this manuscript of yours. It might have – I only say *might* have – possibilities. It would need a good deal of alteration."

Thereafter we went into what seemed to be the routine. I accepted all I was told, signed on a dotted line, and to

my complete stupefaction – got a book actually accepted for publication.

It was the beginning of my career. I had tied myself up to produce five more books, and was quite satisfied to make the sum of twenty five pounds on this first one, *The Mysterious Affair At Styles.*

I did not meet John Lane's nephew Allen until after his uncle died, and when he himself had become a junior member of the firm. I called to protest against a book jacket. It represented a man in pyjamas apparently having an epileptic fit on a golf links – and had no connection with the plot of my book, except that the book's title had been *The Murder On The Links.*

My first impression of Allen Lane has always stayed with me – an impression of vigorous youth and a kind of attractive eagerness – someone very much alive, stretching out towards life and exhibiting a gaiety and friendliness that was immediately endearing.

We became friends at once and I met his two brothers. One of my clearest memories is of those three boys – sharing a flat – making various domestic discoveries - the electric refrigerator, a great novelty, and their over zealous manipulation of its controls resulting in a rabbit frozen so stiff that, – "What can we do with it now?" Their three characters were quite different, but very definitely Allen was in paternal charge of the other two. He regarded his two brothers and his young sister as his responsibility in life. Young and gay as he was, he nevertheless was noticeably *Pere de famille.* It was a touching and lovable attitude. They had enormous fun together.

Brother John was very serious over housekeeping duties and did the washing up with meticulous zeal – and complained bitterly of the other two's untidiness. The link between John and Allen was very close. I think Allen loved John better than anyone in the world and when John was killed in the war, Allen was inconsolable. For a time it seemed to change his character completely. He became in many ways unapproachable.

Sometimes in the early days he and his brothers used to holiday in their boat around the coast of Devon and put into Brixham, and come over and visit us in Torquay.

They gave occasional parties informally in London where we all argued fiercely on subjects of the day. It is long ago now, but I remember Ethel Manin who was a great friend of Allen's and, I think, Rebecca West, airing views together and propounding theories of life. Though never very vocal at parties I much enjoyed listening, among others to Allen himself, who always talked with gusto.

I have often wondered what it was in him that led to his meteoric rise to success.

Certainly he had courage – he was willing to take risks, he had ideas, he had imagination, he had enough knowledge of the ordinary man through his youthful apprenticeship in publishing, to know what the ordinary man wanted, and he knew what he himself planned and wanted to do.

It was a gamble. Rumours went around that he was bankrupt when he went into initial action, and that he had a bare hundred pounds in his pocket. All probably true.

His project had above all the amateur touch – a group of friends, of young men happy and working together and (important, this) enjoying themselves.

Later in life I came across another such a venture – in Damascus when the Nairn Brothers, Gerald and Norman, started the Cross Desert 6 Wheeler Bus Service from Damascus to Baghdad. That too, had the same amateur happy spirit. Some of us, friends of theirs, used to help prepare and pack the lunch boxes late in the evening, ready for the next day's run. It still gives me a thrill to remember those desert journeys from Damascus across the empty desert – the stop at the grim Fort of Rutba, the drive in through the gates under the guns of its armed guard – a few hours rest, and then on through the desert.

The success of Allen Lane and his brothers seems to me to have been of the same kind.

It was a hazardous undertaking – with hardly any solid backing – but it worked.

I am glad that Allen had his triumph. He was a lovable person. In many minor ways he was undependable – when invited to meals he was nearly always late. One learnt to ask him half an hour early! When he got used to that, one raised it to an hour in advance.

Like his uncle, he had a resemblance to Queen Elizabeth the First's "Beloved pirates". He would take gambles and sometimes would be quite un-scrupulous. In early times, before I had acquired the blessing of a literary agent, I used to say suddenly: "Allen, isn't it about a *year* since I've had any royalties from you?"

I can see his face now looking half guilty, half mischievous as he replied: "I wondered whether you'd noticed –"

One quality he never failed in – he had great kindness – and a ready power of compassion which I have known him exercise more than once, sometimes I have thought on unworthy recipients.

After he married his wife, Lettice, I used often to visit them both at their house, Silverbeck. They made a lovely garden there and the noise of Heathrow Airport was not what it was to become later, a torment of screaming jets.

Their three children were lucky to have Allen as a father – the nicest father any children could wish for. He enjoyed doing things with them, made plans every holiday for cycle tours or travels.

It was not parental duty on his part, it was sheer full blooded enjoyment and delight in their company.

Enjoyment of life was charac-teristic of Allen. It was a noticeable trait in his youth – and it increased as he grew older.

He had a natural *flair* for success. It was the secret of what he was able to accomplish. I seldom saw him read a book – and yet he *knew* about books. He sought advice, perhaps, but I doubt if he ever was influenced by advice unless it coincided with his own intuitive judge-ment. When he came on a visit to us, the greater part of each day would always include visits to bookshops in the neighbourhood – questioning, studying trends – finding out where the secret of successful appeal lay.

It was not literature in itself, it was not delight in the printed word that enthralled him, it was the art of publish-ing itself – possibly the sheer science of

Agatha Christie, December 1926.

Popperfoto

it – though I think art is the better word for the way he saw it. He had a feeling for art – in pictures, in carpets, in furniture.

His horizon in publishing widened:– he desired wider territories in which to experiment. Pelicans, Puffins – all the rest of them – archaeology, art, history – he was increasingly conscious of the great richness that can be bestowed through the written word. Since his nature was a generous one, he wanted to bestow these things on an accepting public.

Risks, I am sure, would never deter

him. He would never be one to "play safe". A fortune or bankruptcy? Either way that was life.

When physical health failed him, he accepted fate bravely. There were no complaints or groans. One of the last things he said to me was:

"I don't know how much life I've got left to me, but I'm determined on one thing. I mean to enjoy every moment of it that I possibly can."

A brave man and I think, for most of his life – a happy one.

AGATHA CHRISTIE
Copyright Agatha Christie

The Many Faces Of Poirot

A frame of the credits from the television series, "Poirot".

David Suchet's television portrayal as "Hercule Poirot".

"I've never been an actor to avoid other actor's portrayals," says David Suchet earnestly, "I think that's probably my classical training. You know, to be able to read about or watch another actor's portrayal of Iago or Hamlet is great. I don't sit there and criticise – that doesn't enter into it – I don't sit and think that I can do it better. One accepts that each actor brings something of his own to a part and I learn so much from others."

Forty-three year old David first played Hercule Poirot in 1989 in a £5 million television series of *Poirot* short stories. It was an instant success that was shown in some 35 countries. A second series followed in early 1990 and another series is planned. Serious Christie fans have recognised David Suchet as the image and character that most closely resembles the *little Belgian* of the books and his position would seem to be assured.

Certainly, Poirot has got under David's skin, to the point where he has become almost fanatical about "getting Poirot right and being faithful to the character in the books."

Suchet's attitude towards the retired Belgian police inspector is somewhat parallel to Agatha Christie's. "Poirot can be very irritating" the actor admits. "A real prize nuisance but, paradoxically, he has a great deal of charm and a twinkle. I set great store by that twinkle. I think of it all the time and use it to make Poirot less severe."

Some of the actors who have

"It always seems strange to me that whoever plays Poirot is always an outsize man. Charles Laughton had plenty of avoirdupois, and Francis Sullivan was broad, thick and about 6ft.2in. tall." It always irked Agatha Christie that the character that she had so specifically detailed in her books – a tidy little man of about 5ft.4in. – was so completely ignored by theatrical and film producers. Alas, she did not live to see someone play the role who would probably have delighted her. David Suchet, television's portrayer of the master sleuth, has been described as the 'definitive' Poirot. But he acknowledges a great debt to all the Poirots who came before . . .

tackled Poirot in the past have perhaps lacked this twinkle. It is too easy to let the vanity of the detective take over the characterisation until all that is coming across the footlights is pompous arrogance. It was perhaps the earlier attempts by actors such as Laughton and Sullivan that made Agatha Christie decide to remove Poirot from many of his stories that she adapted for the stage.

Later, Dame Agatha was to thoroughly approve of Albert Finney's portrayal of Poirot in the film of *Murder On The Orient Express*, not the least because the script allowed him to be idiosyncratic and the audience to smile at the fussy little man. Peter Ustinov took over the mantle of Poirot in several cinema and TV films and brought his own brand of gentle humour into the role but, alas, he too is a rather larger portrait than the author had painted.

Curiously enough, David Suchet worked alongside Peter Ustinov in the TV film *Thirteen for Dinner*. "I played the plodding Chief Inspector Japp of Scotland Yard. Little did I know at the time that I'd later be taking over from Peter Ustinov as Poirot. It's extraordinary."

Peter Ustinov as Poirot in the film, "Appointment with Death".

Far from finding the role constricting, Suchet says that he likes being tied down to Agatha Christie's detailed descriptions of Poirot's appearance and behaviour. "It's challenging and a discipline." In fact he takes it so seriously that he has piles of research notes at home and once publicly confessed on a TV chat show that he sometimes phones home to check on the accuracy of certain things. "I want to get Poirot right, so when I play him I give in to his obsessions – neatness and so on. Also, I speak as Poirot all day when filming – I don't slip in and out of the accent."

Suchet wryly admits that he probably identifies quite a lot with the character of Poirot. "My wife says I tend to be over-tidy, I know I'm a bit fastidious, I certainly like my food and I'm afraid if there are three things on a mantelpiece I tend to want to arrange them into symmetrical order."

However, he is very strict about leaving Poirot behind on the film set. And he feels it is extremely important for him to pursue a career as varied as possible. "As long as I can punch in lots of other interesting parts I am quite happy. What I mustn't do is *only* play Poirot."

"I'm lucky really," he reflects. "That when I play Poirot I'm really in disguise – unlike that other famous TV detective, dear Rupert Davies as Maigret, who really played himself and couldn't escape from the role. I mean people don't come up to me in supermarkets and call me Hercule Poirot. Not yet, anyway!" David Suchet smiles and gives a classic example of the famous Poirot "twinkle". Judging by some of his fan mail from all over the world, he could also be the first Hercule Poirot to become the object of female affection!

LYNN UNDERWOOD

Albert Finney in "Murder On The Orient Express".

Agatha's Orient Express

WAGONS-LITS
EUROPEENS

"*All my life I wanted to go on the Orient Express. When I had travelled to France or Spain or Italy, the Orient Express had often been standing at Calais, and I had longed to climb up into it. Simplon – Orient Express – Milan, Belgrade, Stamboul . . .*

Next morning I rushed round to Cook's, cancelled my tickets for the West Indies, and instead got tickets and reservations for a journey on the Simplon-Orient Express to Stamboul; from Stamboul to Damascus; and from Damascus to Baghdad across the desert. I was wildly excited."

Agatha Christie's first journey on the Orient Express came at a time in her life when she was hungry for new and distracting experiences. Her beloved mother had died, her husband had left her and she had suffered a terrible nervous illness. Her daughter had gone back to school and Agatha desperately wanted to get away – to be by herself and to rest. Originally she had planned to go to the West Indies but fate intervened. During a dinner conversation with friends she became entranced by a naval commander's description of Baghdad, and even more enthusiastic when she discovered that one could get there via the Orient Express – the train she had always wanted to travel on. It turned out that fate was indeed dealing her a special pack of cards that evening because it was as a result of this trip to Baghdad that Agatha eventually met Max Mallowan — the man who was to become her second husband.

That first trip on the Orient Express entirely lived up to Agatha's expectations. She had always loved trains and she watched with pleasure as the journey unravelled:

After Trieste we went through Yugoslavia and the Balkans, and there was the fascination of looking out at an entirely different world: going through the mountain gorges, watching ox-carts and picturesque wagons, studying groups of people on station platforms, getting out occasionally at places like Nish and Belgrade and seeing the large

engines changed and new monsters coming on with entirely different scripts and signs.

The people she met were also filed away in that encyclopaedic brain of hers. There was an American missionary lady, a Dutch engineer and "a beaming Turkish lady" who had borne thirteen children. In Stamboul (Istanbul) there was a brief sojourn at the Totaklian Hotel and the introduction to White Russian society, behaving for all the world as though the Revolution in Russia had never taken place. Then, across the Bosphorus by ferry and from Haydarpasa station by the Taurus Express which ambled its way past the Sea of Marmara and the mountains. The crowds on the platforms became more Eastern, the food (to Agatha's dismay) became more unpalatable, but the people on the train become progressively more interesting and the scenery was breathtaking.

Then . . . we came to a halt, and people got out of the train to look at the Cilician Gates. It was a moment of incredible beauty. I have never forgotten it . . . The sun was slowly setting, and the beauty indescribable. I was so glad then that I had come – so full of thankfulness and joy.

Unfortunately, from this point onwards in the journey, Agatha got severely bitten by bed bugs and developed a high fever, which rather took the edge off the experience. But she was better by the time she reached Damascus where she spent three magical days visiting the bazaars and cramming in as much sightseeing as she could. From there on, the journey across the desert was by bus and she regretfully said goodbye to the train.

After her marriage to Max Mallowan, Agatha was to undertake the Orient Express journey many times – they even travelled part of the way on the train for their honeymoon – and although some of the experiences (yet more bed bugs) were less than wonderful, Agatha never lost her fascination for the train. It was 1928 when she took that first journey and in 1934 her book *Murder on the Orient Express* was published.

Although Agatha does not herself refer to the grand style, sumptuous food and wine that the train offered, the Orient Express was, nevertheless noted for it. Since its maiden voyage on October 4, 1883 from Paris to Constantinople (now Istanbul) it had been a byword in luxury – marble bath fixtures, the finest linen for the beds, crystal and brass light fittings, handmade lace antimacassars and velvet seating. The dining car was fully staffed by waiters in impressive livery and served only the finest food and wines. It was the favourite mode of travel for the wealthy – royalty, actors, diplomats, financiers, even spies.

Agatha based her book on two real events – totally separate, but which she blended together with the imaginative skill that was her trademark. First, was the Lindbergh kidnapping. The world-famous aviator Charles Lindbergh became the target of a vicious kidnap plot in the year before Agatha started writing her book. His two-month-old baby was kidnapped from the family home in New Jersey and a huge ransom demanded. The ransom was paid but the baby was killed. In 1933 one Bruno Hauptmann was executed for the crime, although he claimed innocence until the end. The second event took place before that in January 1929. That winter was one of the harshest on record – all of Europe was covered in snow and ice and the Orient Express became marooned in a huge snowdrift just inside the Turkish border and was cut off from the rest of the world for six days.

In her book, the travellers on the train all have mysterious pasts and the train is marooned in a snowdrift on the Bulgarian-Yugoslavian border, at which time the murder takes place. Hercule Poirot is, by fortunate coincidence, a traveller on the train – returning from a successful assignment in Syria.

The book was an outstanding success. The reviewer in the New York Times said *"Although the murder plot and the solution verge upon the impossible, Agatha Christie has contrived to make them appear quite convincing for the time being, and what more can a mystery addict desire?"*

The exotic glamour of the setting of the train and the cast of characters (A Russian Princess, a Count and Countess and assorted mysterious foreigners) made the book a definite target for the film industry. However, it was not until 1963 that anyone ventured to propose it and, at that point Agatha firmly refused. MGM had bought the rights to several of her books and had signed Margaret Rutherford to play Miss Marple, a choice that Agatha Christie was not entirely happy with. Nevertheless she recognised that Miss Rutherford was making a valiant attempt and, although she was nothing like Agatha's vision of Miss Marple, Agatha said nothing as she did not wish to hurt the actress' feelings. MGM also displayed the prevailing tendency of British cinema at the time to turn Agatha's stories into farces by injecting comedy scenes which were not in the original books. When MGM proposed to write a screenplay of *Murder on the Orient Express* and substitute Miss Marple for Hercule Poirot, Agatha rebelled. She said to her agent *"The book took a lot of careful planning and technique and to have it possibly transformed into a rollicking farce with Miss Marple injected into it and probably acting as the engine driver, though great fun no doubt, would be somewhat harmful to my reputation!"*

She refused to sell any more film rights to MGM. No-one was going to turn her beloved *Orient Express* into the setting for a low comedy.

However, in the 1970s, Lord Brabourne, a successful independent film producer and his partner, Richard Goodwin, decided that they would like to film *Murder on the Orient Express*. They had the backing of the giant EMI Corporation and Lord Brabourne also had the added advantage of being the son-in-law of Lord Mountbatten, who was an avid Christie fan and had corresponded with the writer on several occasions, although they had never actually met.

Brabourne and Goodwin had also recently produced *The Tales of Beatrix Potter*, a daring film which featured the dancers of The Royal Ballet Company in magical animal costumes and the whole film was bathed in the pastel colours which so strongly and faithfully represented the books of Beatrix Potter. Fortunately, Agatha had loved the film and therefore was persuaded to at least listen to Brabourne's ideas. Over lunch he explained to her that he and his partner wished to lovingly recreate the atmosphere of the original Orient Express (they had located a coach in France which they intended to rebuild in England) and to fill the film with internationally famous stars clothed in elegant costumes. The whole film, he assured her, would be a serious and stylish masterpiece. It took several months of negotiations but finally she was persuaded. *Murder on the Orient Express* could make the journey to the big screen.

Paul Dehn wrote a wonderful script and this script was sent to director Sidney Lumet. After a long silence, Lumet agreed and suggested Sean Connery for

The cast of the film in the recreated carriage of "The Orient Express".

one of the roles in the film. (Lumet had worked with Connery on a previous film) Brabourne and Goodwin were overjoyed. The next problem was to find someone to play Hercule Poirot. They made what was to some, a rather curious choice – Albert Finney. True he was box office magic at the time, but Finney playing Poirot? Many remained to be convinced. Nevertheless, Finney loved the script and accepted, and his name, along with Sean Connery's and Sidney Lumet's got, in Brabourne's words *"everyone queuing up to be in the picture."* Certainly the galaxy of stars finally assembled was impressive. Aside from those mentioned the cast included Lauren Bacall, Martin Balsam, Ingrid Bergman, Jacqueline Bisset, Jean-Pierre Cassel, John Gielgud, Wendy Hiller, Anthony Perkins, Vanessa Redgrave, Rachel Roberts, Richard Widmark, Michael York, Colin Blakely, George Colouris and Dennis Quilley.

The train was restored to its former glory at Elstree Studios. Tony Walton was the production designer and it was he who brought the style and elan to the sets and costumes. He was eventually to win an Oscar for Best Costumes.

Most of the location work took place in France, Turkey and Borehamwood and the film took just 42 days to shoot. In France, the director and cast found themselves assembled and praying for snow, which was essential to the plot. Fortunately, the night before the scheduled shooting was to take place, snow fell like a thick blanket and, with aid of some judicious shovelling, the Orient Express was truly snowbound for the relevant scenes.

The film won three out of the seven British Film Awards that year – Best Picture; Best Actor (Albert Finney) and Best Actress (Wendy Hiller). Albert Finney had proved to be a masterly Poirot, padded and mannered and entirely convincing. Few filmgoers will ever forget the scene where he retired to bed for the night with his pomaded hair and moustache both encased in hairnets – a wonderful touch of typical Poirot vanity!

In the United States the film was nominated for six Oscars – eventually gaining just one – Best Supporting Actress (Ingrid Bergman).

The budget for the film went up and up and up, until it reached a limit of £4¹⁄₂ million – the largest budget Brabourne and Goodwin had ever worked with. However, it turned out to be the most successful wholly British-financed film made to date.

The producers took the brave step of allowing Agatha Christie and her husband to see the "rough edit" of the film and they were rewarded when she thoroughly approved. It was, in fact, the first film of one of her books that she was totally satisfied with. Lord Mountbatten persuaded her to come to the Royal premiere and the Queen, in her brief chat with the authoress, reinforced the idea that all the Royal Family were Agatha Christie fans.

The review in The Times said *"Sidney Lumet's adaptation of Murder on the Orient Express is a deliberate period pastiche . . . It is touchingly loyal to Mrs. Christie and to the period . . . It stays precisely at the level of Agatha Christie, demands the same adjustments, the same precarious suspension of belief."*

LYNN UNDERWOOD

Her Esoteric World Of Invention

Agatha Christie's ideas far exceeded even the enormous number of stories that she produced in her lifetime. Her mind, beneath that placid exterior must have been constantly teeming with plots, counter plots, suspects and motives. A glance at her carefully preserved notebooks, in her old house Greenway, now occupied by her daughter and son-in-law, shows that her trains of thought were often quite erratic – skipping from one exotic subject to another. The notes were often quite brief, in a kind of Christie speedwriting, aide memoires only for her and quite meaningless to anyone else, except the interested researcher who recognises the odd components of, now, well-known books.

Agatha herself, constantly bemoaned her lack of organisation . . .

. . . what I invariably do is lose the exercise book. I usually have about half a dozen on hand, and I used to make notes in them of ideas that struck me, or about some poison or drug, or a clever little bit of swindling that I had read about in the paper. Of course, if I kept all these things neatly sorted and filed and labelled it would save me a lot of trouble. However, it is a pleasure sometimes, when looking through a pile of old notebooks, to find something scribbled down, as: "Possible plot – do it yourself – Girl and not really sister – August" with a kind of sketch of a plot. What it's all about I can't remember now: but it often stimulates me, if not to write that identical plot, at least to write something else.

Agatha's method of working was to spend about eighty percent of her time sorting out the details of her plots in her head and then the other twenty percent was spent on a furious burst of writing. As her son-in-law Anthony Hicks comments "You never saw her writing. I would come to Greenway for a visit and

> "Plots come to me at such odd moments: when I am walking along the street, or examining a hat shop with particular interest, suddenly a splendid idea comes into my head, and I think 'Now that would be a neat way of covering up the crime so that nobody would see the point'. Of course, all the practical details are still to be worked out, and the people have to creep slowly into my consciousness, but I jot down my splendid idea in an exercise book."

Tony Martin

she was the perfect hostess, always there, always joining in. She never, in the whole time I knew her, suddenly got up and said 'I must go and write now' and shut herself away, like other writers do." Yet her output of books was prodigious throughout her life.

The oddest things stimulated Agatha into a book.

I had another idea after going to a performance by [the actress] *Ruth Draper. I thought how clever she was and how good her impersonations were; the wonderful way she could transform herself from a nagging wife to a peasant girl kneeling in a cathedral. Thinking about her led me to the book "Lord Edgeware Dies."*

Urged by her husband, Archie Christie, to write a second book, after the modest success of her first, Agatha considered the matter.

Supposing I did – what should it be about?

The question was solved for me one day when I was having tea in an A.B.C. Two people were talking at a table nearby, discussing somebody called Jane Fish. It struck me as a most entertaining name. I went away with the name in my mind. Jane Fish. That, I thought, would make a good beginning to a story – a name overheard at a tea shop – an unusual name, so that whoever heard it remembered it. A name like Jane Fish, or perhaps Jane Finn would be even better. I settled for Jane Finn and started writing straight away.

The book was to be called *The Secret Adversary.* Her third book, *Murder on the Links* was prompted by a news-

The Orient Express in 1884 during the first year of its operation.

paper story – often something which, in an oblique way, triggered a Christie plot. This particular news story was a murder which had taken place in France. A man had supposedly been killed by masked intruders, while his wife and mother were tied up. However, it transpired that the police believed that there had been no masked men and that, in fact, the wife had committed the murder. This struck Agatha as a good plot on which to weave her own story ...

starting with the wife's life after she had been acquitted of the murder. A mysterious woman would appear somewhere, having been the heroine of a murder case years ago.

There were less obscure "triggers" for plots, of course. Agatha's first journey, alone, on the Orient Express and the characters she observed on her journey, were ingredients for *Murder on the Orient Express*. Her travels in the Middle East with her second husband, Max Mallowan, provided rich material for several books, among them *Death on the Nile*, *Murder in Mesopotamia* and *They Came to Baghdad*.

Acquaintances and friends often appeared in Christie novels, although Agatha rarely took the whole personality into the plot, just bits and pieces, such as her first husband's business associate Major Belcher, whose pompous turn of phrase and unscrupulous nature surfaced in the guise of Sir Eustace Pedlar, the likeable rogue in *The Man in the Brown Suit*. Many of the people Agatha met as a result of accompanying her second husband on archaeological digs, surfaced in her books.

Often, the Christie notebooks were just ways of working out her indecisions

John E. May

about something, like a title.
One notebook reads:

Title?

Dooms Caravan
Swallows Nest
Postern of Fate
Disaster's Caravan
Fort of Fear

Pass not beneath, O Caravan, or pass not singing
Have you not heard
That silence where the birds are dead yet
Something pipeth like a bird?
Pass out beneath, O Caravan
Doom's Caravan, Death's Caravan

She eventually decided on *Postern of Fate*, which was published in 1973.

Always attracted by the supernatural (a legacy from her mother who was interested in such things too), another Christie notebook reads:

Possibilities and ideas.
Stories Ghost or such type.

The Dressmaker's Doll
The Harlequin Tea Set
*The Last Seance**

The Spanish Horse

*Medium – Blood mother siezes child that is materialized – medium dies as a result.

New one – haunted house – ghost is dog, cat or both?

The Dressmaker's Doll, *The Harlequin Tea Set* and the *Last Seance* were all eventually published in short story collections.

In 1963, her notebook read:

West Indian book – Miss M ? Poirot?
2 pairs husband and wife
B & E apparently devoted – actually B and G (Georgina) had affair for years ...
Old "frog" Major knows – has seen him before – he is killed.

One year later *A Caribbean Mystery* was published and we learnt that Agatha had decided on Miss M rather than Poirot and the "old frog" Major was indeed the first murder victim of the plot.

Another notebook reads:

Miss M
Train coming from London to Reading?
Man strangles a woman
The train was?
3.55
3.19

We know, of course, that she settled on the 4.50 From Paddington.

But let Agatha Christie have the last word on this subject:

Some of my books satisfied and pleased me. They never pleased me entirely, of course, because I don't suppose that is what one ever achieves. Nothing turns out quite in the way that you thought it would when you are sketching out notes for the first chapter, or walking about muttering to yourself and seeing a story unroll."

LYNN UNDERWOOD

The Gentle

Joan Hickson as Miss Marple – "Body In The Library".   © BBC

But Determined Character

"*Murder At The Vicarage* was published in 1930, but I cannot remember where, when or how I wrote it, why I came to write it, or even what suggested to me that I should select a new character – Miss Marple – to act as the sleuth in the story. Certainly at the time I had no intention of continuing her for the rest of my life. I did not know that she was to become the rival of Hercule Poirot."

In her autobiography Agatha Christie gives a great insight into how she shaped the character of Miss Marple and it is only fitting that we should let her continue that description . . .

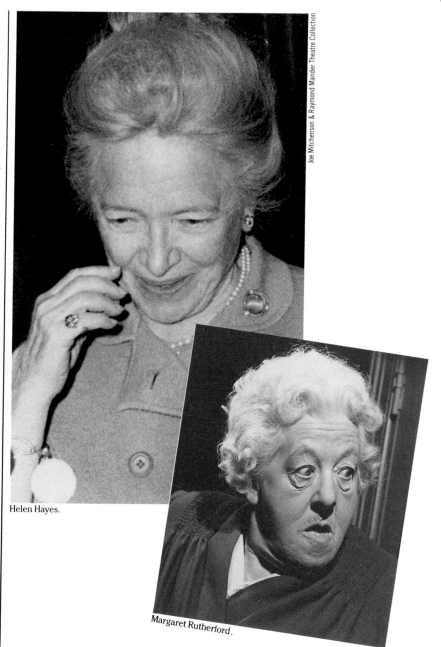

Joe Mitchenson & Raymond Mander Theatre Collection

Helen Hayes.

Margaret Rutherford.

"Miss Marple insinuated herself so quickly into my life that I hardly noticed her arrival. I wrote a series of six short stories for a magazine and chose six people whom I thought might meet once a week in a small village and describe some unsolved crime. I started with Miss Jane Marple, the sort of old lady who would have been rather like some of my grandmother's Ealing cronies – old ladies whom I have met in so many villages where I have gone to stay as a girl. Miss Marple was not in any way a picture of my grandmother; she was far more fussy and spinsterish than my grandmother ever was. But one thing she did have in common with her – though a cheerful person, she always expected the worst of everyone and everything and was, with almost frightening accuracy, usually proved right . . .

Anyway, I endowed Miss Marple with something of Grannie's powers of prophecy. There was no unkindness in Miss Marple, she just did not trust people. Though she expected the worst, she often accepted people kindly in spite of what they were."

Agatha Christie portrayed Miss Marple in *Murder at the Vicarage* as someone with a sweet and gentle appearance, faded blue eyes and snowy hair. Agatha herself described her in her autobiography as "dear, pretty, old, fluffy". She viewed everything and assessed everyone from the vantage point of her garden in the village of St Mary Mead and her passions in life were knitting and gossip – not that she spoke much but invariably probed gently and encouraged others to tell all.

Alas, once again, as with Hercule Poirot, Agatha was to be disappointed at theatrical and film directors' inability to stick to the true character of her creation. Some very odd actresses played Miss Marple, from Gracie Fields (complete with broad Lancashire accent) to a very formidable and cheerful Margaret Rutherford, who really was so much more at home in St Trinian's films than in St Mary Mead.

By one of those curious quirks of fate, in 1945, Agatha after viewing the premiere of her play *Apointment With Death* at the Piccadilly Theatre in London, wrote to a young actress who appeared in the play as the character Miss Price.

"Dear Miss Price,

How nice of you to send me a telegram! I thought the play went well – but the notices have been pretty bad in the Telegraph and The Herald.

I was at the Guinea Pig last night and enjoyed it enormously –

Going back to Devon on Satur- day where I shall rest up and have a think. Come and have lunch with me – I will call you to play my "Miss Marple" one day, if I can find time to write another play – too many domestic chores."

The young actress who received that letter was none other than Joan Hickson – regarded today as the quintissential Miss Marple.

"I never dreamt I would play Miss Marple," says Joan Hickson now, from her home in an English village, not unlike St Mary Mead. "I'd forgotten the letter until my daughter found it two or three years ago."

Gracie Fields.

Joan Hickson as Miss Marple – "4.50 From Paddington".   © BBC

Joan Hickson came to British television screens as the elderly lady detective in 1984 and then became an international success the following year.

Miss Hickson was no stranger to Agatha Christie adaptations, having played throughout her career in several of the author's plays and even two of the films – the prestigious 1937 film *Love From A Stranger* starring Basil Rathbone and the 1962 disappointment *Murder She Said* with Margaret Rutherford as Miss Marple.

"I wasn't influenced by other portrayals at all," says Miss Hickson (which is probably just as well, since none have portrayed Miss Marple as remotely like the character in the books). "I have always seen Miss Marple as typically English, very quiet and resolute but down to earth. She notices everything that goes on.

"I know what English village life is like," she adds, "and I think Agatha Christie described it perfectly. Living in a village one gets to know everything and that's exactly how Miss Marple got her 'intelligence'. You can never shock her but she's very upright, without being judgemental, and is always on the side of justice."

Joan Hickson has done 10 Miss Marple TV films now, which makes her far and away the front runner in the Miss Marple stakes. Angela Lansbury was given a rather dismal stab at the role in the film *The Mirror Crack'd* but the scriptwriters did not do Miss Marple justice that time. Nonetheless, many people took to Miss Lansbury in the role

and she subsequently went on to star in a Christie-type spin-off called *Murder She Wrote*. Another valiant portrayal of recent times has been in two American film adaptations, *A Caribbean Mystery* (1983) and *Murder With Mirrors* (1985), where Helen Hayes played Miss Marple. She was physically like the sweet old lady of Agatha's vision and her character was pleasingly quiet and determined. Agatha probably would have approved, but for the fact that the producers chose to update the Christie stories to the present day and this rather took the edge off things for diehard Christie fans, who

like period authenticity as well as a good thriller.

No, Joan Hickson remains the firm favourite with millions of viewers and she is pleased about that. "I've loved it more than anything I've ever done," she says, "It was all filmed in the lovely setting of the village of Nether Wallop, the other members of the cast were lovely and it always seemed to be fine weather. And it is so lovely to play a character who is regarded all over the world with such affection."

LYNN UNDERWOOD

An Extraordinary Diversity Of Characters

The Agatha Christie WHO'S WHO

More than 2,000 colourful characters from the world of Agatha Christie, completely cross-referenced and elegantly illustrated. Compiled by Randall Toye and published by Frederick Muller.

Agatha Christie is probably best known for her two dominant creations – Hercule Poirot and Miss Marple. But, in over 50 years of writing some 66 mystery novels and one hundred and forty seven short stories, she created many memorable characters. Here, Lynn Underwood looks at some of the other Christie sleuths.

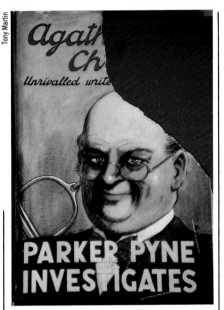

N o-one is unimportant in a Christie novel. Victim, suspect, witness, gossip, policeman, detective – all have a part to play in the puzzle which has to be solved.

Critics of the Christie style of writing have accused her of 'formula' writing, stating that she always used the same types of characters in the same claustrophobic setting, such as a house party, river boat or train – all are gathered together in a situation begging for a murder, everyone is suspect, all the characters are larger than life. But, in fact, one glance at the masterly work *The Agatha Christie Who's Who* compiled by Randall Toye and published by Frederick Muller Limited, shows that, amongst over 2,000 characters who are deemed by the editor worthy of potted biographies, there is an extraordinary diversity.

True, there is more than a handful of doctors who crop up in Christie books (but then doctors can commit murder so easily can't they?), similarly there are

military gents, lords and ladies, maids and butlers, spinsters and widows – but so there are in life – or at least there were in Agatha Christie's life. Her critics tend to bemoan her tendency to set her novels in middle class or upper class society, but this criticism is hardly worthy of comment. Agatha Christie wrote about the society with which she was familiar, as did Sir Arthur Conan Doyle and Dorothy L. Sayers. Sticking to what one knows hardly makes a story less valid.

Agatha Christie's power of observation were acute. Often she absorbed the nuances of the character of a real-life person and attributed them to one of her

characters. For example, the irritating, vain and pompous Major Belcher, her first husband's business colleague formed the basis for Sir Eustace Pedlar in the book *The Man in the Brown Suit*.

Perhaps the author's greatest ingenuity was reserved for her detectives. No-one could ever accuse Agatha Christie of sticking to a formula there – they were all so different. The pedantic little Belgian, Hercule Poirot, was just about as different as anyone could be from the quietly nosy English spinster, Jane Marple. Agatha herself wrote in her autobiography "People never stop writing to me nowadays to suggest that Miss Marple and Hercule Poirot should meet – but why should they? I am sure they

would not enjoy it at all. Hercule Poirot the complete egoist, would not like being taught his business by an elderly spinster lady. He was a professional sleuth, he would not be at home at all in Miss Marple's world."

Poirot was Agatha's first and, possibly greatest invention. Her second book *The Secret Adversary* featured a pair of sleuths who were very much drawn from real life. Tommy and Tuppence Beresford were a pair of 'bright young things' whom the reader meets just after the First World War. Tuppence worked in the Volunteer Aid Detachment during the war (as did Agatha) and Tommy was in the Royal Flying Corps (as was Agatha's husband Archie). They were totally reflective of the period in which the book was published (1922) – two young upper middle class people who, we read between the lines, had a gay old time before the war at house parties and dances, find themselves after the war disorientated by the huge change in society, drawn together as survivors of a generation where very few survived, needing work and unable to find any. The pair decide to hire themselves out as 'adventurers' and then find themselves caught up in an international intrigue.

Agatha turned to Tommy and Tuppence several times throughout her writing career, in 1929 for the book of short stories *Partners in Crime*, 1941 for the book *N or M?*, 1968 for *By the Pricking of my Thumbs* and finally, in 1973 for *Postern of Fate*. Fortunately, unlike Poirot or Miss Marple, the Beresfords started out rather young, so by the time Agatha injected them into their last adventure it was possible to age them gracefully into grandparents, but still with a keen sense of adventure.

After *The Secret Adversary*, Agatha wrote several Poirot books and some which contained 'one-off' sleuths, unfortunate bystanders who happened to get drawn into a mystery and end up solving it, like Anne Beddingfield in *The Man in the Brown Suit* (1922). The next significant detective to be added to the Christie stable was in 1930 when *The Mysterious Mr. Quin* was born. He was one of her favourite characters because he allowed her to indulge in her fascination with the supernatural and her love for the characters of the Commedia Dell'Arte (Harlequin, Columbine, Pierrot etc.). Mr. Harley Quin was indeed a quirky invention.

In the Quin stories it is actually Mr. Satterthwaite who is the sleuth. He is a rather suave bachelor with an abiding interest in other people's affairs. Mr. Harley Quin is his 'helper'. He is not real to anyone but Mr. Satterthwaite and the reader. He appears and disappears unexpectedly, often with strange lighting effects and he injects into the situation precisely what Mr. Satterthwaite needs in order to reach a deduction. It is a pure piece of theatricality but it works. The Quin mysteries are all confined to short stories originally published in 1930 but they resurfaced in two editions of American collections in 1950 and 1951.

Agatha then created Miss Marple in 1930 for *Murder at the Vicarage* and for the next couple of years she seesawed between Poirot and Miss Marple in her books. Then, in 1934, she wrote *Parker Pyne Investigates*. Although Mr. Pyne only featured in one book of short stories he was yet another of Agatha Christie's delightful hiccups of imagination which led into a totally different sphere of mysteries. Mr. Parker Pyne was primarily a sleuth for the lovelorn. Most of his cases concern affairs of the heart which he attracts by means of an advertisement in the personal columns of the newspapers which reads *"Are you happy? If not, consult Mr. Parker Pyne"*. Mr. Pyne is gentlemanly, concerned and discreet. He does not take centre stage like Hercule Poirot, he is content to work in the background, towards a happy ending for the parties concerned.

The Parker Pyne stories are also notable because they feature Ariadne Oliver and Felicity Lemon in cameo appearances. The redoubtable Miss Lemon is Mr. Pyne's secretary before eventually becoming Hercule Poirot's

One of Agatha's favourite characters Mr Harley Quin.

secretary (Agatha often liked to recycle characters she was particularly fond of) and Ariadne Oliver helps Mr. Pyne, later becomes a companion of M. Poirot and then becomes an amateur sleuth in her own right.

From 1934 until the war, Agatha wrote almost exclusively Poirot books, apart from one diversion in 1939 for *Murder is Easy*, when she introduced another of her hapless 'passers-by', one Luke Fitzwilliam, who unwittingly becomes involved in a mystery and, with the help of Superintendent Battle of Scotland Yard, solves it.

Superintendent Battle features as the lone sleuth in the 1944 book *Towards Zero*. It is, in fact, a rare occasion when a policeman is permitted to work unaided by any private detective and the book received mixed reviews, although Agatha Christie regarded it as one of her best plots.

In 1945 she wrote *Sparkling Cyanide* which featured Colonel Johnny Race as the detective. Colonel Race had previously been a sidekick of Hercule Poirot's in two other novels *Cards on the Table* and *Death on the Nile*, replacing the faithful Captain Hastings, who was at Poirot's side for most of his adventures. Colonel Race also appeared in the very early novel "The Man In The Brown Suit" without M. Poirot. Colonel Race is a dependable sort with an impeccable background in the British Secret Service so he is well equipped to deal with shady goings-on. *In Death on the Nile* he appears to be rather plodding, suffering from the 'Holmes/Watson' syndrome of playing second fiddle to the brilliant 'little grey cells' of the magical Belgian. But in *Sparkling Cyanide* he is allowed to shine. Unfortunately it was the last time that Agatha Christie used him in one of her books. Like Superintendent Battle, who featured in five Poirot novels before starring alone in *Towards Zero*, he is retired after his hour of glory.

Perhaps this is the place to honour the most long-suffering of all the Christie characters – Chief Inspector James Japp of Scotland Yard, who has the misfortune to play the stooge of officialdom to Hercule Poirot in no less than twelve short stories and sixteen books. Like Inspector Lestrade who followed in the trail of Sherlock Holmes, Inspector Japp bears the brunt of the withering condescension of the egotistical Poirot.

Finally, we have Mrs. Ariadne Oliver, who appeared in earlier Poirot and

Miss Marple.

Parker Pyne stories but did most of her own sleuthing in novels that were published in the 1950s and '60s. Described as having a 'booming contralto voice'…'Windswept grey hair'…and an 'eagle profile', Mrs. Oliver is a writer of crime novels. There has been some debate as to whether Agatha Christie intended Ariadne Oliver to be a parody of herself. Certainly Mrs. Oliver's personality is far more forceful than Agatha's ever was, but Mrs. Oliver does have a passion for munching apples while writing (which Agatha did) and Mrs Oliver's main creation is a frightful Finnish detective who alternatively infuriates and charms his creator (shades of Poirot?).

There are many other Christie characters that one could draw from their settings and admire like jewels but, where to draw the line? When researching for his book *The Agatha Christie Who's Who* Randall Toye drew up an initial catalogue of over 7,000 listings and eventually pared it down to 2,000.

How can one person create so many captivating characters? The answer is that Agatha Christie was a great observer of human nature. As she said in her autobiography *"It is no good thinking about real people – you must create your characters for yourself. Someone you see in a tram or a train or a restaurant is a possible starting point, because you can make up something for yourself about them."*

LYNN UNDERWOOD

Agatha's signature for Mary Westmacott was deliberately different from her Agatha Christie signature.

The Secret Of Mary Westmacott

Reading in hindsight, about Agatha Christie's diverse talents as a writer – poet, novelist, scriptwriter – it would be surprising if she had not branched out from the world of detective fiction and written novels in some other genre. Agatha's daughter, Rosalind Hicks, takes up the story and explains the secret of Mary Westmacott . . .

A s early as 1930, my mother wrote her first novel using the name "Mary Westmacott". These novels, six in all, were a complete departure from the usual sphere of Agatha Christie "Queen of Crime".

The name Mary Westmacott was chosen after some thought. Mary was Agatha's second name and Westmacott the name of some distant relatives. She succeeded in keeping her identity as Mary Westmacott unknown for fifteen years and the books, much to her pleasure, were modestly successful.

Giant's Bread was first published in 1930 and was to be the first of six books under this nom de plume. It is a novel about Vernon Deyre, his childhood, his family, the two women he loved and his obsession with music. My mother had some experience of the musical world having been trained as a singer and a concert pianist in Paris when she was young.

She was interested in modern music, and tried to express the feelings and ambitions of the singer and the composer. There is a lot about childhood and the First World War taken from her own experiences.

Her publishers, Collins, were not very enthusiastic about this change of direction in her work as she was at this time becoming quite well known in the world of detective fiction. They needn't have worried. In 1930 she also published *The Mysterious Mr Quin*, and *The Murder at the Vicarage* – Miss Marple's first book. During the next ten years there followed no less than sixteen full length Poirot stories including such titles as *Murder On The Orient Express, The ABC Murders, Death On The Nile,* and *Appointment With Death*.

Her second Mary Westmacott book *Unfinished Portrait* was published in 1934. It also relied a lot on her own experiences and early life. In 1944 she published *Absent In The Spring*. She wrote in her autobiography:

"Shortly after that, I wrote the one book that has satisfied me completely. It was a new Mary Westmacott, the book that I had always wanted to write, that had been clear in my mind. It was the picture of a woman with a complete image of herself, of what she was, but about which she was completely mistaken. Through her own actions, her own feelings and thoughts, this would be revealed to the reader. She would be, as it were, continually meeting herself, not recognising herself, but becoming increasingly uneasy. What brought about this revelation would be the fact that for the first time in her life she was alone – completely alone – for four or five days.

"I wrote that book in three days flat ... I went straight through ... I don't think I have ever been so tired ... I didn't want to change a word and although I don't know myself of course what it is really like, it was written with integrity, with sincerity, it was written as I meant to write it, and that is the proudest joy an author can have."

I think *Absent In The Spring* combines many talents from Agatha Christie, the detective story writer. It is very well constructed, compulsive reading. You get a wonderfully clear picture of all the family from the thoughts of one woman alone in the desert – really quite a triumph.

In 1947 she wrote *The Rose And The Yew Tree*. This was a great favourite of hers and of mine too. It is a haunting and beautiful story. Strangely enough Collins didn't like it and as they hadn't been very kind about any of the Mary Westmacotts, she took it to Heinemann who published this and her last two books – *A Daughter's a Daughter* (1952) and *The Burden* (1956).

The Mary Westmacott books have been described as romantic novels but I don't think that is really a fair assessment. They are not 'love stories' in the general sense of the term, and they certainly have no happy endings. They are, I believe, about love in some of its most powerful and destructive forms.

The possessive love of a mother for her child, or a child for its mother in both *Giant's Bread* and *Unfinished Portrait*. The battle between the widowed mother and her grown-up daughter in *A Daughter's a Daughter*. A girl's obsession with her younger sister in *The Burden* and the closeness of hate to love – the Burden in this story being the weight of one person's love on someone else.

Mary Westmacott never enjoyed the same critical acclaim as Agatha Christie, but the books achieved some recognition in a minor way and she was pleased when people enjoyed them – she was able to fulfil her wish to write something different

ROSALIND HICKS

Tony Martin

The Complete

Agatha Christie Book List

DATE	UK TITLE	USA TITLE
1932	*The Blue Geranium*	
	The Companion	
	The Four Suspects	
	A Christmas Tragedy	
	The Herb of Death	
	The Affair at the Bungalow	
	Death by Drowning	
1933	Lord Edgware Dies	Thirteen at Dinner
	The Hound of Death	(not published in USA)
	The Hound of Death	
	The Red Signal	
	The Fourth Man	
	The Gypsy	
	The Lamp	
	Wireless	
	The Witness for the Prosecution	
	The Mystery of the Blue Jar	
	The Strange Case of Sir Arthur Carmichael	
	The Call of Wings	
	The Last Seance	
	S.O.S.	
1934	Murder on the Orient Express	
1934	The Listerdale Mystery	(not published in USA)
	The Listerdale Mystery	
	Philomel Cottage	
	The Girl in the Train	
	Sing a Song of Sixpence	
	The Manhood of Edward Robinson	
	Accident	
	Jane in Search of a Job	
	A Fruitful Sunday	
	Mr Eastwood's Adventure	
	The Golden Ball	
	The Rajah's Emerald	
	Swan Song	
1934	Why Didn't They Ask Evans?	The Boomerang Clue
1934	Parker Pyne Investigates	Mr Parker Pyne, Detective
	The Case of the Middle Aged Wife	
	The Case of the Discontented Soldier	
	The Case of the Distressed Lady	
	The Case of the Discontented Husband	

Tony Martin

Tony Martin

DATE	UK TITLE	USA TITLE
1934	The Case of the City Clerk The Case of the Rich Woman Have you got everything you want? The Gate of Baghdad The House at Shiraz The Pearl of Price Death on the Nile The Oracle at Delphi	
1935	Three Act Tragedy	Murder in Three Acts
1935	Death in the Clouds	Death in the Air
1936	The A.B.C. Murders	
1936	Murder in Mesopotamia	
1936	Cards on The Table	
1937	Dumb Witness	Poirot Loses a Client
1937	Death on the Nile	
1937	Murder in the Mews Murder in the Mews The Incredible Theft Dead Man's Mirror Triangle At Rhodes	Dead Man's Mirror
1938	Appointment with Death	
1938	Hercule Poirot's Christmas	Murder for Christmas
1939	Murder is Easy	Easy to Kill
1939	Ten Little Niggers	Ten Little Indians (later retitled And Then There Were None, in UK & USA)

DATE	UK TITLE	USA TITLE
1939	(not published in the UK)	The Regatta Mystery and other Stories *The Regatta Mystery* *The Mystery of the Bagdad Chest* *How Does Your Garden Grow?* *Problem at Pollensa Bay* *Yellow Iris* *Miss Marple Tells A Story* *The Dream* *In a Glass Darkly* *Problem at Sea*
1940	Sad Cypress	
1940	One, Two, Buckle My Shoe	The Patriotic Murders
1941	Evil Under The Sun	
1941	N or M?	
1942	The Body in the Library	
1942	Five Little Pigs	Murder in Retrospect
1943	The Moving Finger	
1944	Towards Zero	
1945	Death Comes as the End	
1945	Sparkling Cyanide	Remembered Death
1946	The Hollow	Murder After Hours
1947	The Labours of Hercules *Foreword* *The Nemean Lion* *The Lernean Hydra* *The Arcadian Deer* *The Erymanthean Boar* *The Augean Stables* *The Stymphalian Birds* *The Cretan Bull* *The Horses of Diomedes* *The Girdle of Hippolyta* *The Flock of Geryon* *The Apples of the Hesperides* *The Capture of Cerberus*	
1948	Taken at the Flood	There is a Tide
1948	(not published in the UK)	The Witness for the Prosecution and other Stories *The Witness for the Prosecution* *The Red Signal* *The Fourth Man* *S.O.S.* *Where there's a Will* *The Mystery of the Blue Jar* *Philomel Cottage* *Accident* *The Second Gong*

DATE	UK TITLE	USA TITLE
1949	Crooked House	
1950	A Murder is Announced	
1950	(not published in the UK)	*Three Blind Mice and other Stories* *Strange Jest* *The Tape Measure Murder* *The Case of the Perfect Maid* *The Case of the Caretaker* *The Third Floor Flat* *The Adventure of Johnnie Waverly* *Four and Twenty Blackbirds* *The Love Detectives*
1951	They Came to Baghdad	
1951	(not published in the UK)	The Under Dog and other Stories *The Under Dog* *The Plymouth Express* *The Affair at the Victory Ball* *The Market Basing Mystery* *The King of Clubs* *The Submarine Plans* *The Adventure of the Clapham Cook* *The Cornish Mystery* *The LeMesurier Inheritance*
1952	Mrs McGinty's Dead	
1952	They Do It With Mirrors	Murder with Mirrors
1953	After the Funeral	Funerals are Fatal
1953	A Pocket Full of Rye	
1954	Destination Unknown	So Many Steps to Death
1955	Hickory, Dickory, Dock	Hickory, Dickory, Death
1956	Dead Man's Folly	
1957	4.50 From Paddington	What Mrs McGillicuddy Saw!
1958	Ordeal by Innocence	
1959	Cat Among the Pigeons	
1960	The Adventure of the Christmas Pudding *The Adventure of the Christmas Pudding* *The Mystery of the Spanish Chest* *The Under Dog*	(not published in USA)

DATE	UK TITLE	USA TITLE
1960	*Four and Twenty Blackbirds* *The Dream* *Greenshaw's Folly*	
1961	The Pale Horse	
1961	(not published in the UK)	*Double Sin* *Double Sin* *Wasp's Nest* *The Theft of the Royal Ruby* *The Dressmaker's Doll* *Greenshaw's Folly* *The Double Clue* *The Last Seance* *Sanctuary*
1962	The Mirror Crack'd from Side to Side	
1963	The Clocks	
1964	A Caribbean Mystery	
1965	At Bertram's Hotel	
1966	Third Girl	
1967	Endless Night	
1968	By The Pricking of My Thumbs	
1969	Hallowe'en Party	
1970	Passenger to Frankfurt	
1971	Nemesis	

DATE	UK TITLE	USA TITLE
1971	(not published in UK)	*The Golden Ball* *The Listerdale Mystery* *The Girl on the Train* *The Manhood of Edward Robinson* *Jane in Search of a Job* *A Fruitful Sunday* *The Golden Ball* *The Rajah's Emerald* *Swan Song* *The Hound of Death* *The Gypsy* *The Lamp*

DATE	UK TITLE	USA TITLE
		The Strange Case of Sir Arthur Carmichael *The Call of Wings* *Magnolia Blosson* *Next to a Dog*
1972	Elephants Can Remember	
1973	Postern of Fate	
1974	Poirot's Early Cases *The Affair at the Victory Ball* *The Adventure of the Clapham Cook* *The Cornish Mystery* *The Adventure of Johnnie Waverly* *The Double Clue* *The King of Clubs* *The Lemesurier Inheritance* *The Lost Mine* *The Plymouth Express* *The Chocolate Box* *The Submarine Plans* *The Third Floor Flat* *Double Sin* *The Market Basing Mystery* *Wasps Nest* *The Veiled Lady* *Problem at Sea* *How Does Your Garden Grow?*	
1975	Curtain	
1976	Sleeping Murder	
1979	Miss Marple's Final Cases	

OTHER BOOKS

PUBLISHED AS MARY WESTMACOTT

1930	Giant's Bread
1934	Unfinished Portrait
1944	Absent in the Spring
1948	The Rose and the Yew Tree
1952	A Daughter's a Daughter
1956	The Burden

PUBLISHED AS AGATHA CHRISTIE

1924	The Road of Dreams (poetry)
1973	Poems
1977	An Autobiography

PUBLISHED AS AGATHA CHRISTIE MALLOWAN

1946	Come Tell Me How You Live
1965	Star Over Bethlehem (poems and children's stories)

Tony Martin

Agatha And Max

On her first trip to Baghdad, Agatha Christie met Leonard Woolley and his wife Katharine and became friendly with them. Leonard, later Sir Leonard, was the leader of an archaeological dig at Ur and he and his wife invited Agatha to stay with them and to return the following year. This she did, and on this second visit she met Leonard Woolley's assistant, who had been absent through illness on her first visit. His name was Max Mallowan and he was to become her second husband.

Sir Max Mallowan, in his own autobiography "Mallowan's Memoirs" (published by Collins) describes their first meeting and the blossoming relationship that ensued;

"The year 1930, my fifth and penultimate season at Ur, was of crucial importance in my life, for it was the year of my marriage...

When Agatha came down to stay [at Ur] in March of that year Katherine Woolley in her imperious way ordered me to take her on a round trip to Baghdad and see something of the desert and places of interest on the journey. Agatha was rather nervous at this request and afraid that it might cause me displeasure when I might be looking forward to journeying home on my own. However, I found her immediately a most agreeable person and the prospect pleasing.

We set off together and inspected the ruins at Nippur, greatly impressed by their starkness, the gaunt ziggurat and the eerie nature of the site, which was

Agatha at the time of her marriage to Max, 1930.

Our guide had hardly gone for five minutes, incidentally a very handsome Bedouin guide in the uniform of the desert police with a long flowing kefiyah, than there passed by on this lonely track an old fashioned 'T' Ford filled to the brim with passengers. They stopped and all fourteen of them got out and lifted our car bodily out of the sand; a minor miracle. Praising God we drove to Kerbela where we spent the night in the police station and were each allotted one cell, one for Agatha and one for myself. My last duty for the night was to escort her by the light of a police lantern to the lavatory. We had breakfast in the prison where I remember that one of the policemen recited to us "Twinkle, twinkle Little Star" in Arabic. The mosque at Kerbela was of singular beauty and the tiles a wonderful sky-blue that one does not easily forget. We reached Baghdad in good heart and arrived at the Maude Hotel where we had a very pleasant stay in that primitive inn. After being stuck in the sand on the way to Kerbela we never looked back and I don't think I guessed that the short journey to Baghdad would lead to a longer union which was destined to last for the best part of fifty years. We travelled home together part way on the Simplon Orient Express after accompanying the Woolleys as far as Aleppo where we parted company from them. Our journey on the Taurus Express at the end of March was wholly enjoyable and gave me the firm intention of seeking Agatha's hand when we reached home.

We were married on 11 September 1930."

Agatha Christie recalled in her autobiography, more detail of the journey home with Max. Agatha, the Woolleys and Max had reached Athens when a telegram arrived saying that her daughter Rosalind was dangerously ill with pneumonia. Agatha had to get home as soon as possible...

"...Walking along the street, half-dazed with shock, I put my foot into one of those square holes in which trees seemed eternally to be planted in the streets of Athens. I sprained my ankle badly, and was unable to walk. Sitting in the hotel, receiving the commiserations of Len and Katherine, I wondered where Max was. Presently he came in. With him he had two good solid crepe bandages and an Elastoplast. Then he explained quietly that he would be able to look after me on the journey home and help

one of the oldest in Sumer. We spent a strange night at Diwaniyah with the political officer, Ditchburn, who was extremely rude about all archaeologists and obviously displeased at having us to stay. Thereafter we made a trip to Nejeif, a wonderful old walled town, one of the Holy Pilgrim cities of the Shiahs. There we were not allowed to go in a mosque, but we saw one of the last horse-drawn trams: I have only seen two others, the first as a boy at Kew and the second in San Francisco. From Nejeif we motored on to Kerbela where we were to spend the night, visiting on the way the lovely Ummayed castle of Ukhaidir, so well described by Gertrude Bell in *Amurath to Amurath*. Walking around the parapets of those high battlements was a terrifying experience if you had no head for heights, but I led Agatha round them all,

by hand, and she confided herself to me without too much trepidation.

After visiting the castle, as it was a boiling hot day, we decided to have a bathe in a salt lake nearby, but in doing so the car became inextricably stuck in the sand and looked as if it would never get out. Fortunately we had with us a Bedouin guard supplied by the police at Nejeif to see us on the way to Kerbela and after praying to Allah he set off to make the forty mile journey on foot in order to get help while we resigned ourselves patiently to a very long wait. I remember being amazed that Agatha did not reproach me for my incompetence in leading the driver to get stuck in the sand, for had I been accompanied by Katharine Woolley that is what would have happened, and I then decided that she must be a very remarkable woman.

me with my ankle.

'But you are going up to the Temple of Bassae' I said 'Weren't you meeting somebody?'

'Oh I've changed my plans' he said 'I think I really ought to get home, so I will be able to travel with you. I can help you along to the dining car or bring meals along to you, and get things done for you.'

It seemed too marvellous to be true. I thought then, and indeed have thought so ever since, what a wonderful person Max is. He is so quiet, so sparing with words of commiseration. He does things. He does just the things you want done and that consoles you more than anything else could. He didn't console me over Rosalind or say she would be all right and that I mustn't worry. He just accepted that I was in for a bad time. There were no sulpha drugs then, and pneumonia was a real menace.

Max and I left the next evening. On our journey he talked to me a great deal about his own family, his brothers, his mother, who was French and very artistic and keen on painting, and his father, who sounded a little like my brother Monty – only fortunately more stable financially…

…I remember little of that journey with Max except his extraordinary kindness, tact, and sympathy. He managed to distract me by talking a good deal about his own doings and thoughts. He bandaged my ankle repeatedly, and helped me along to the dining car, which I do not think I could have reached by myself, especially with the jolting of the Orient Express as it gathered strength and speed. One remark I do remember. We had been running alongside the sea on the Italian Riviera. I had been half asleep, sitting back in my corner, and Max had come into my carriage and was sitting opposite me. I woke and found him studying me, thoughtfully. 'I think' he said 'that you have a really noble face.' This so astonished me that I woke up a little more. It was a way I should never have thought of describing myself. A noble face – had I? It seemed unlikely. Then a thought occurred to me. 'I suppose' I said 'that is because I have a Roman nose.' Yes, I thought, a Roman nose. That would give me a slightly noble profile. I was not sure I quite liked the

Agatha Christie playing the piano for her husband Max Mallowan, the archaeologist, at their home, Greenway House, Devon.   Popperfoto

idea. It was the kind of thing that was difficult to live up to. I am many things: good-tempered, exuberant, scatty, forgetful, shy, affectionate, completely lacking in self-confidence, moderately unselfish but noble – no, I can't see myself as noble. However, I relapsed into sleep, rearranging my Roman nose to look its best – full-face rather than profile."

Forty six years later, as Max Mallowan was putting the finishing touches to his autobiography, his beloved Agatha died, 'peacefully and gently'. He wrote this Epilogue in his book;

"She had been failing for some time and death came as a merciful release, though it has left me with a feeling of emptiness after forty-five years of a loving and merry companionship. Few men know what it is to live in harmony beside an imaginative, creative mind which inspires life with zest. To me, the greatest consolation has been the recognition, which has come from many hundreds of letters, that admiration was blended in equal measure with love – a love and happiness which Agatha radiated both in her person and in her books…"

Agatha Among The Archaeologists

Popperfoto

Agatha Christie and husband Professor Max Mallowan on the first stage of their flight to make archaeological excavations in 1950.

Agatha Christie's second marriage, to archaeologist Max Mallowan, was a happy and long union of two professionally satisfied people. Agatha became a prolific and well-regarded author during their marriage, Max was eventually knighted for his services to archaeology. Agatha found Max's work fascinating. She loved the Middle East and accompanied him every year to his digs. She took up photography and became a useful helper to her husband. Their partnership was truly productive and fulfilling.

Donald J. Wiseman, now Emeritus Professor of Assyriology in the University of London, accompanied Agatha and Max to the digs between 1950 and 1963. He was then Assistant Keeper of the British Museum and an epigraphist. (It was his job to read all the inscriptions found on artifacts at the site.) In this article he recalls Agatha amongst the archaeologists – her energy and her enthusiasm.

Agatha sat contentedly in the battered, bulgy and creaking wicker-work arm-chair in the small room built as an extension to the mud-brick expedition house at Nimrud. The rough concrete floor was relieved by a few rush mats over which were spread brightly coloured kelims. The window had no curtains so she could gaze over the rolling plain which hid the outer city edged by low mounds covering the ancient walls. In the far corner stood pyramidal mounds (Tulul el 'Azar) which a few years later were to yield their secrets as the Royal Arsenal (Fort Shalmaneser). This was the site of the

Max in the porch of the expedition house at Ur 1926.

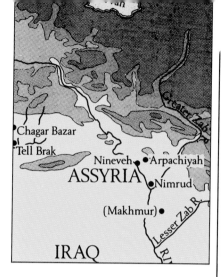

Expedition house at Chagar Bazar.

Assyrian military capital of ancient Kalhu (biblical Calah) which Agatha had visited twenty years earlier while they were working at Nineveh and she had persuaded Max that it was worth exploring, not the least because of its setting and carpet of spring flowers. On the home-made table, not so sturdy as that in the main dig work room, lay her typewriter and a flurry of papers anchored down by some potsherds and a pile of paperback books. These had to be swept into a gaily coloured Arab tin trunk as protection from a dust storm or from the rust which during a heavy rainstorm spattered down from the corrugated sheets stretched over saplings which supported the mud roof.

For almost thirty years Agatha had accompanied Max on his annual archaeological expeditions since they had first met on Leonard Woolley's excavations at Ur and had shared the hardships of life in the field. These early days she described in her entertaining book *Come, Tell Me How You Live* (1946), still one of the best about life on an archaeological survey and dig. Max added his own reminiscences in *Mallowan's Memoirs* (Collins, 1977). Agatha recalled many an experience – kept awake by fleas, mice, rats or, bats in the high tower of the rented house at Chagar Bazar, before Max had built his dig house there. She certainly had her likes and dislikes, human and circumstantial. "I might have been murdered," said Agatha, upbraiding Max for leaving her alone for thirty minutes once while they were counting out from a suitcase, kept under Agatha's bed, the silver coins then used for paying the labourers' wages. Nor did she like the physical discomfort of a long ride on a mule.

At Nimrud the archaeological team slept in tents pitched outside the expedition house. Agatha too. This was her preference to the suggestion that one of the old iron beds be brought into her room. The room had been built in a day with the help of the diminutive carpenter I had brought out from Mosul. He worked with primitive bow-drill and tools, little changed from those used by the Assyrians 2700 years before when they had built the royal palace complex we unearthed. Agatha's room, she said, cost her fifty dinars (£50) but my own notebook of costs indicated it was less than that. Inside the door was a nail on which Agatha would hang her floppy hat and often her soaking macintosh. Outside the door I penned an inscription in the Assyrian cuneiform script — 'Agatha's house' (*bît Agata*). Someone added 'Apply here if you want to get rid of your wife ... mother-in-law ...', but this was soon removed to conserve the anonymity of the place. Here Agatha started to write her *Autobiography* (1977).

A few years later we made the men bring up surplus inscribed bricks from the excavations and with them I constructed a bathroom near her room. Using an old tin Victorian hip bath filled by a procession of servants was preferable to ablutions in the confines of a tent. Agatha seemed unimpressed with the layout which I had designed to encourage anyone in the bath to read the boastful inscriptions on the bricks – claims of earlier inhabitants of the mound. She was delighted when Max found a real Assyrian bathroom of King Adad-nērāri III with its bitumen covered floor and upturned waterpots still there. However, we all preferred the luxury of a real bath offered by European friends whenever we got into Mosul.

Nothing could mitigate the hazardous journey along the ramparts to the

The staff at Ur in 1926: Back row, left to right: Max, Hamoudi, Leonard Woolley, Katherine Woolley and Father Burrows (epigraphist).

rough sack-enclosured open air toilet. In bad weather Max was as anxious about this as for all Agatha's welfare. Today Agatha's room and the adjacent bathroom are sometimes photographed by visitors and pointed out to be part of the ancient ruins!

The inscription for Agatha's house in Assyrian Cuneiform script, created by Donald Wiseman.

Burnt brick Ziggurat at Ur, showing the north-east face with triple staircase. Built by Ur-nammu about 2100 BC.

Agatha played a full part on each of 'the expeditions when she accompanied Max annually, save in the war years, between 1932-60. She would emerge perspiring from a morning's work in the small unventilated darkroom, for she took many of the best photographs. She generally oversaw the welfare of the household and its provisioning. To hear her brief the cook or the servant Michael was an ear- and eye-opener. Sending the driver Petros off on a laundry and shopping trip usually ended with ". . . and don't forget the cream." Our high standard of living and health was not a little due to Agatha's watchful concern and to her use of tax-allowances (given for obtaining 'local colour and background' for her writing) put into entertainment. She was inherently shy except with friends and members of the team who had learned not to discuss her writing.

Many were the visitors attracted to this internationally famous site. Agatha sat at the head of the long table behind her tea or coffee pot dispensing hospitality to high and low. For government and diplomatic officials as well as fellow archaeologists, native and foreign, headed for the site. More than 1500 arrived in one season at Nimrud, including army officers on manoeuvres, chil-

Excavating at Nimrud. Max is in the foreground.

dren by the bus load, church dignitaries or even locals arriving on donkeys to look for work.

The longer visits of Allen and Lettice Lane were well remembered – he air-mailed out whole Stilton cheeses to us from Penguin at Harmondsworth. Also Ernest and Dora Altounyan from Aleppo who supplemented Agatha's own knowledge of medicines, learned as a dispenser in two World Wars. Ernest prescribed 'horse-medicine' as more effective than the Epsom Salts we were giving for the stubborn cases of constipation among the labourers. His wife Dora spent the time painting sketches of the camp site and work in progress. Agatha was always more interested in the living than the dead who surrounded us.

Agatha was an indefatigable traveller and experienced in searching the numerous ruin-mounds (*tells*) at which we would stop during any 'rest day' excursion. She would turn over the scattered fragments with her stick and collect the essential sherds by which the site could be dated. She seemed to have a preference for Ninevite V wares and the spring flowers she collected en route. She was a good example of patience during the inevitable delays in travel or when waiting for hours to be feasted by a sheikh. She was always willing to drop her reading or knitting when there was a major find. I have vivid recollections of her using one of her knitting-needles when cleaning a fine and intricate ivory piece found down a well and of her commandeering all our towels to cover the earliest writing boards ever found and then watering them hourly to prevent them drying out too quickly.

Max proudly acknowledged her

efforts in his detailed report on the excavations, *Nimrud & Its Remains* (Collins, 1966) which he dedicated to her, and in his *Memoirs*. He would point out those objects in the British Museum which Agatha had repaired, including the fine polychrome Arpachiyah pottery they had found on an earlier dig.

Agatha was conservative in many ways. It took a lot of persuasion to let us introduce an electric generator to provide light in the workroom and to the end we used parrafin pressure lamps for most purposes, the generator being tucked away off behind an earth dump to prevent its spluttering disturbing the quiet of the desert night. However, conversation with Agatha heading the table was certainly unrestricted. We all shared our hopes and fears and frustrations in a friendly and comradely atmosphere over lengthy evening meals after a long day's work.

One difficult year she came to the rescue by donating the manuscript of *A Pocket Full of Rye* to help the expedition survive financially. Various episodes grave and gay were, like Easter and birthdays, commemorated by a poem or 'odd ode' which she would read. A long discussion on the behaviour of our guard dog and his bark *ruh* – ('go away') *rah* ('he has gone') resulted in an *Ode to Toto in Calah*. No member of the expedition was spared but all were rewarded by the presentation of the appropriate manuscript. No wonder that the now dwindling band of her archaeological colleagues and contemporaries drink a heartfelt toast each year 'To Max and Agatha' when they dine together.

PROFESSOR DONALD J. WISEMAN

Beit Agatha (Agatha's House)

Ashfield House

"Looking back over the past, I become increasingly sure of one thing. My tastes have remained fundamentally the same. What I liked playing with as a child, I like playing with as an adult. I have liked playing Houses, for instance."

So Agatha Christie wrote in her autobiography. As a child, playing with her dolls' house was her favourite indoor pastime. Most of her pocket money was spent on furnishing it and she pleaded to be allowed another one. Her mother did not think little girls should have two dolls' houses but suggested that a cupboard was used and by putting her dolls' house on top, the young Agatha had a six storeyed house. Of particular enjoyment was house moving when a stout cardboard box was pressed into service as a furniture van – useful practice for her many moves in later life!

Agatha was born at Ashfield, Barton Road, in Torquay, Devonshire, a large house typical of the villas built for the middle class families of the late Victorian era. She attributed her happy childhood, in part, to having *"a home and garden that I loved"*. In the last book she wrote. *Postern of Fate*, there is a description of a garden and lean-to greenhouse containing a rocking horse and other toys which is almost identical to the description of the greenhouse and garden at Ashfield in her autobiography.

Despite the family's reduced income, after her father's death, Agatha was still living at Ashfield with her mother when she met Archie Christie, and continued to live there after her marriage in 1914. When Archie was posted to the Air Ministry in London she joined him to start their married life together in a tiny flat in Northwick Terrace, St John's Wood.

Agatha went back to stay at Ashfield in 1919 for the birth of her daughter, Rosalind and, a month after the birth, left Rosalind with her mother and a nurse whilst she returned to London to look for a larger flat. She found one fairly quickly at 25 Addison Mansions, behind Olympia. *"The flat was filled with particularly hideous furniture, and had some of the most sentimental pictures I have ever seen."* But it was large, with four bedrooms and two sitting rooms (all for 5 guineas a week!). Archie, Agatha, Rosalind, a nurse and maid all moved in to start family life there. But soon an unfurnished flat had to be found. After a hectic couple of months, they were fortunate in obtaining one in the adjoining block. Agatha and Archie furnished this flat with some *"good modern furniture for Rosalind's nursery and new beds from Heals"*, tables, chairs, cabinets and linen from Ashfield and chests of drawers and old-fashioned wardrobes bought "for a song" from sales. Archie and Agatha lived in Addison Mansions until early in 1924 when they moved to Sunningdale in Berkshire, some 30 miles south west of London.

Scotswood was a large Victorian house divided into four flats. The ground floor had already been let but the Christies had the choice of the upstairs ones, with the use of the garden for Rosalind to play in.

As their financial position became more assured, Agatha and Archie looked around Sunningdale for a house to buy. Archie lived and breathed golf and was keen to buy a house on the Wentworth estate which was being built around two golf courses, but the cheapest house there was far beyond their means. After having looked at innumerable houses, they chose one which was near the station, *"a sort of millionaire-style Savoy suite transferred to the country and decorated regardless of expense."* Despite it having a reputation for being an

Styles house.

unlucky house they bought it and renamed it Styles, after the title of Agatha's first published novel.

Unfortunately Styles proved again to be an unlucky house and the Christie's marriage ended. Agatha moved into a flat in Kensington High Street with Rosalind and her faithful secretary-governess and friend, Carlo Fisher, while Archie continued to live at Styles for a time, but it was soon put on the market. After a holiday in the Canary Islands Agatha moved to a flat in Chelsea with Rosalind and Carlo.

Winterbrook House, Wallingford.

Cresswell Place.

Greenway House, Devon.

which she was to own for the rest of her life. 22 Cresswell Place, Chelsea was a mews house which, with the help of a builder, she substantially altered to make a comfortable, if rather cramped home. She was generous with her houses and lent them to friends willingly. In the summer of 1929 she lent Cresswell Place to Sir Leonard and Lady Woolley, archaeologists whom she had met in the Near East the previous winter. They invited her to their archaeological dig at the end of the next season to travel back with them through Syria and Greece. It was on this second visit to Ur that Agatha met Max Mallowan. They were married in September 1930 and when Max returned to Ur after their honeymoon, Agatha set about furnishing a new house they had bought in Campden Street, London.

In 1934 Max and Agatha decided Ashfield was too far to travel for weekends, so they started looking for a cottage in the Thames Valley. In December they bought Winterbrook, a delightful, small Queen Anne house about a mile out of Wallingford and with a river frontage. To Agatha's joy there was a huge Cedar of Lebanon under which, on hot days, she envisaged having tea. They had to leave for Syria as soon as they had signed the various papers and did not see Winterbrook again for about 9 months. On their return Agatha enjoyed decorating this house, the drawing room in her favourite colour, pale mauve, with white woodwork, curtains and furnishings.

Another house they bought at about this time was, 48 Sheffield Terrace, Campden Hill, London which had large, well-proportioned rooms. Having been brought up in a house with spacious rooms Agatha had felt the lack of space in both Cresswell Place and Campden Street. Sheffield Terrace was the first house where Agatha had a room of her own in which to work. In the past this had always caused consternation when an interviewer wanted to photograph her

"at her work". On being asked where she wrote, she would reply "Oh, anywhere." As Agatha recounts in her autobiography "All I needed was a steady table and a typewriter".

Whilst staying at Ashfield in the summer of 1938 (no longer a peaceful home on the edge of fields, but now with small houses surrounding it and a large school blocking the view of the sea), Agatha saw an advertisement for a house she remembered visiting as a child. Greenway House had always been considered by Agatha's mother to be the most perfect house on the River Dart. The original white Georgian mansion had had extensive Victorian additions, but the gardens were beautiful, so, encouraged by Max, Agatha sold Ashfield and bought Greenway for the amazing sum of £6,000. Set in 33 acres of grounds it had a boathouse, covered swimming pool (refilled each high tide), and battlements at the spot where Sir Walter Raleigh was reputed to have landed on his return from the New World. Aided by a young architect friend they removed most of the Victorian additions to the house and Agatha set about decorating it with her usual enthusiasm. Greenway, its grounds and boathouse are the setting for her novel, *Dead Man's Folly*.

During the Second World War, Greenway was requisitioned by the Admiralty for use by the officers of an American flotilla. A historic memorial of the United States Navy's occupation is a fresco around the walls of the library which depicts all the places that particular flotilla had visited. It remains there still, but unfinished. Before the sailors could join the fresco so that it totally encircled the room, they were posted overseas.

Max, unable at first to join the Services, was working for a Turkish

Relief Project in London and once Greenway had been let, Agatha joined him there. As their own houses and apartments were all unavailable they lived first in a flat in Half Moon Street – in the only building left standing after a recent bombing raid – they moved to a service flat in Park Place off St James Street. After their tenants in Sheffield Terrace gave up the lease. Max and Agatha moved back into there until it was damaged by a landmine. Agatha then sent all her furniture to be stored in the squash court at Winterbrook and she and Max moved to a flat in Lawn Road, Hampstead. Max had, to his joy, finally got a job at the Air Ministry and shortly after they moved to Lawn Road he was posted to the Middle East. Agatha, meanwhile, resumed her old profession as a dispenser, working part-time in University College Hospital.

The Admiralty gave up Greenway in February 1945 and Max returned soon after to work at the Air Ministry in London. They left the flat in Lawn Road and moved into Cresswell Place, but spent time at both Greenway and Winterbrook tidying up the gardens. Before leaving for their first post war archaeological dig they moved from this mews house which they let, to a flat in Swan Court, off King's Road Chelsea. During their first season at Nimrud, they lived in part of a house owned by a Sheikh, but for the following season they had a house built. To this a year or two later Agatha added, at her own expense, a room in which she could work. One of the archaeological team placed a notice on the door – *Beit Agatha*, Agatha's House. This room was simply furnished with rush mats, a couple of colourful rugs, some Iraqi paintings, a table, an upright chair, an easy chair and, of course, a typewriter. When not in the Middle East they spent their time between Winterbrook, Greenway and Swan Court. Cresswell Place was usually rented or lent to friends.

It was at Winterbrook in 1965 that Agatha Christie completed her autobiography, started at Nimrud in 1950, in which she wrote: *"I can see plainly now that I have continued to play houses ever since. I have gone over innumerable houses, bought houses, exchanged them for other houses, furnished houses, decorated houses, made structural alterations to houses. Houses! God bless Houses!"*

FRANCES M NALDRETT

Agatha Christie - A Legend For A Grandmother

Agatha Christie with grandson Mathew, 1955.

In reality, of course, she was nothing like that. She was an intensely shy, very private kind of person, who listened more than she talked, who saw more than she was seen, and whose perception, humour and enjoyment of living was in many ways the opposite of what you might expect from the nature of her stories. Her family life was what she prized most – I think she regarded our summers together as a reward in part for the completion of another Christie for Christmas which had usually taken place by May or June each year and in part as relaxation from the strenuous archaeological tours she undertook with her husband Max Mallowan most springs during the 1950s. We all looked forward to them, I as a schoolboy more than most.

At the time these were golden summers and in retrospect they lose none of their attraction. Imagine the scene – a beautiful white Georgian house on the river Dart, tennis and cricket on the lawn, scrumptious teas and the company of a united and devoted family. I used to call my grandmother Nima which I suppose was my first inarticulate attempt at Grandma when I was very young. At any rate it became a universal family name which somehow seemed appropriate. My first memories concern rushing downstairs far too early in the morning with my two soft cuddly elephants Butterfly and Flutterby (they had huge pale blue ears) and being told fantasies about their life in the jungle by Nima in her bed. I suspect that if the detective story had not got such a hold on her by that stage she would have tried her hand at children's stories – they were always different and riveting to me. In the afternoons we used to walk down to Nima's riverside boathouse and watch the pleasure boats sail up the river Dart. They came from Brixham and Torquay –

"Agatha Christie – she was your grandmother?" I have lost count of the number of times this has been said to me in varying tones of incredulity, awe or reverence. Most people seem to be quite comfortable with the image of her as a famous writer and household name but somehow feel less at home having to come to terms with her as a wife, mother and grandmother. People feel that the writer of over eighty crime stories can have had time for nothing else, or maybe they look at me and reckon I was lucky to survive almost thirty-five years close association with the inventor of so many ingenious murders. Once they have recovered from the shock, my inquisitors reveal a new characteristic – uncontrollable curiosity. They try and force me to remember a notebook on every dining-table, poison in every meal, conversations composed in riddles, dramatic denouements on every day out from school – surely she must *have been like that?*

the *Kiloran, Western Lady, Torbay Princess* and the *Pride of Paignton*. Then up the hill for cream teas which Nima enjoyed even more than I did – she used to drink hers from a huge cup with *Don't be greedy* written on the outside; an injunction she never showed any sign of obeying. There were day trips to Dartmoor in an old black Humber with bucket seats (and later an old Phantom III Rolls Royce – a hugely impractical car).

There were peaches for dinner on magnificent plates each decorated with a different fruit; for some years these were orchestrated by a butler called Gowler (a professional conjurer in his spare time) who used to hide the face of the plates with a linen napkin and finger-bowl and rigorously only allow each guest his favourite plate once a week. Nima's favourite was the fig, but even she was rationed and I can remember the tension

as the finger-bowls and napkins were raised and an assortment of cries of triumph and groans of despair were heard ("Oh I hate the blackcurrants. Not the gooseberries *again!*"). But Gowler was always the only winner. It was an idyllic atmosphere for a child, and no wonder I always cried when I left.

But, one may ask, did "work" in the shape of writing novels and, plays not intrude at all on this domestic family scene. Yes, of course, it did – but always in a strictly controlled and highly civilised way. I have since learnt that invitations to Greenway by my grandmother's colleagues were highly prized and everybody who came entered into the spirit of the occasion. I remember Peter Saunders, the impresario who produced *The Mousetrap* came frequently – he was very popular with me as a regular purveyor of medium-pace off-breaks at cricket on the lawn but I also

remember spirited arguments between Nima and him on the plausibility of certain plots or parts of plots to a stage audience. These discussions were also notable because I do occasionally remember Peter winning a point – but not very often! I remember Allen Lane of Penguin Books who arrived in a Bentley Coupe with a 3 on its numberplate (I was collecting numbers) and Billy Collins, with great big bushy eyebrows, arriving almost apologetically with a typescript under his arm which, like most publishers, he wanted back corrected the day after tomorrow.

Best of all I remember the year when Nima read us a chapter or two of *A Pocketful of Rye* after dinner each night. It must have been 1953 and I can remember the scene as if it were yesterday. All the family sitting round the drawing-room at Greenway, coffee cups empty, a little cigar smoke rising from my grandfather's cigar, mauve chintzy covers on the chairs and a piano in the corner of the room. Nima sat in a deep chair with a light directly above her and her spectacles, a strange butterfly shape, were pushed slightly forward. After every session, except the first two or three, we were all invited to guess the identity of the murderer. Was it Adele or Elaine? (poisoning is a woman's weapon perhaps?) Or, maybe not, because Percival or Lancelot might have done it. Or what about the sinister Miss Armsbottom? Two reactions I remember clearly: my grandfather Max usually finished his cigar and went to sleep during the reading, waking up with a start when we were all guessing. He then consistently and obstinately plumped for the most unlikely and impossible suspect and went to sleep again. My mother, on the other hand, maintained the solution was, of course, crystal clear to anyone with a grain of intelligence and that the plot was so transparent that it was hardly worth inflicting it on the public. However, she was not prepared to be more explicit. There was, of course, a serious purpose behind these highly enjoyable occasions. Nima was anxious to try out her book on a live audience which enabled her to test its plausibility and its plot. Needless to say Max and my mother in their wholly different ways guessed correctly and infuriated the rest of us!

The early 1950s were the period when Agatha Christie plays first made their mark in the West End of London,

Grandson, Mathew in 1989.

starting of course with *The Mousetrap* in 1952. Hence Peter Saunders frequent appearances at Greenway. *The Mousetrap* rights were given to me around my ninth birthday but I do not remember being aware of this until much later. Anyway, I am sure I received from Nima a more orthodox birthday present as well! What I do remember is that the advent of the plays in London made Nima noticeably more famous in the eyes of my schoolmates particularly. To begin with, of course, *The Mousetrap* was not particularly sensational and nobody thought it would do better than have "a nice little run" (Nima's actual words). But *Witness for the Prosecution* which followed it two years later was a spectacular success with Patricia Jessel playing the lead role. The first-night audience stamped and shouted their approval and demanded that Nima appear on stage. Eventually, and very reluctantly, she did and I honestly believe it was nearly the only public appearance of her life which she actually enjoyed. She described it as "rather thrilling really!" All these events were naturally reported in the papers and were perhaps the beginning (or certainly at least the resurgence) of Agatha Christie as something more than an ordinary thriller writer. I received a certain amount of reflected glory at school, particularly when my signed copy of the annual new book arrived and in common with all books received at school, went to be vetted for suitability by the headmaster. Mine took longer than normal to return and I did occasionally wonder whether Nima had overstepped the limits of violence acceptable to the headmaster. I need not have worried – I later discovered that the headmaster's wife always insisted on reading them before handing them back to me!'

During the late 1950s and early 1960s the play anniversaries mounted up – three Agatha Christie plays running simultaneously in the West End and *Mousetrap* landmark after *Mousetrap* landmark – five years, one thousand performances, beating the venues record set by other plays etc. Peter Saunders never failed for an excuse for a party nor was he unaware of the resultant publicity but it reflected too on Nima and the popularity of her books. At that time I was at boarding school not far from Nima's house at Wallingford near Oxford. This was a delightful house within a short walk of the Thames and I often used to take friends from school there. We used to chug up and down the Thames in a small motor-boat, play squash in an old-fashioned court in the grounds and stuff ourselves full of chicken or roast beef at lunchtime, joined enthusiastically by Nima and Max. I don't know what my friends expected before they met her, but all were impressed by her modesty, friendliness and above all by the interest she unfailingly took in what *they* were doing at the time.

Nima's other passion (apart from writing and reading, that is) was music. I was told that when she was young she seriously considered a career as a concert singer, abandoning it only because the onset of nerves was so great whenever she sang in public. Certainly I remember her singing snatches of early twentieth century songs, accompanying herself on the piano, and excerpts from Gilbert and Sullivan. Best of all, I remember two trips we made together in search of opera, which was a passion of mine too. When I left school we visited Bayreuth together, the home of Wagner. Nima, I remember, travelled under an assumed name to avoid being recognised, a subterfuge which lasted all of twenty-four hours. However, an accommodation was reached with our hotel manager who agreed to fend off all fans provided Nima agreed to sign paperback books for an hour after breakfast each morning. This did not interfere with music loving and our worship of Wagner and his characters continued. Nima and Max were fascinated with the atmosphere of Bayreuth which was almost religious in character. Parsifal particularly impressed them with its bare sets and almost Nordic costumes, and nearly five hours of complete reverence. For myself, once I had got used to sitting for long periods on cane chairs, it was an unforgettable experience. I still possess a beautiful leather-bound compilation of the programmes of the operas we saw, given to me by Nima for my birthday on our return.

The next year we went to Salzburg, accompanied this time by two Oxford friends, Ellis Wisner and Roger Angus. Here the deal was simple – Nima and Max paid for the opera tickets and dinner afterwards and we were in charge of transport in our battered Vauxhall Victor estate car. Nima was staying in an excellent hotel, whilst we were camping. The first night we almost were refused admissions to the hotel such was our grimy state having driven, I think, from Verona, and several nights later we almost were thrown out of the camping site for wearing a dinner-jacket! However, all this was incidental to the splendour of Herbert Von Karajan in his glory, not to mention memorable daytime trips in the Austrian countryside, where I remember Ellis being dumbfounded at Nima's willingness to argue the toss with him about nineteenth-century philosophy, which he was reading at Oxford.

Usually during the winter Nima and Max spent time with us in Wales, my father's family home. Once we had a fete, and my mother somehow persuaded Nima to come and sit in a chair and sign books. Inevitably, word got out of this rare public appearance and an ordinary village fete (on a mercifully fine day) turned into a stampede. It was made more interesting by the fact that two weeks earlier Nima had broken her right wrist and signed all the books left-handed – a typically warm-hearted and determined gesture.

Here she met my other Welsh-Canadian grandmother, another remarkable character. I remember driving over for tea (thin cucumber sandwiches) and remarking that I was sorry we were late but we had been held up by road works on the way, where they were trying to repair a particularly dangerous corner.

"They're wasting their time" said Granny Nora "the gypsies cursed that corner years ago when old Harbour (a particularly notorious local character) turned them off the land." Thus did Nima have the legend of Gypsy's Acre, on which the book *Endless Night* was based. This for something more than personal reasons has always remained one of my favourite books, the more remarkable since it is a book that depends for its success on the accurate perception of young people's hopes and fears in a modern society, a remarkable perception considering that Nima was over seventy when she wrote it.

Hanging over the fireplace at my

Guinness watched incredulously by the rest of us. Nima sat in a chair for the sittings owned by an art dealer friend of mine, James Kirkman, who organised the event and I am told he has left me the chair in his will!

Towards the end of her life occurred the first of two great explosions which I believe have helped the immortalisation of Nima's books. This was the film explosion. It was not that films of the books had not been made before – notedly perhaps a marvellous film of *Witness for the Prosecution*, directed by Billy Wilder and starring amongst others Charles Laughton and Marlene Dietrich – but there hadn't been many distinguished ones until John Brabourne and Richard Goodwin produced *Murder on the Orient Express*. A marvellous cast was assembled, Sidney Lumet directed a magical script written by the late Paul Dehn and the result had people queuing in the snow in New York in the winter of 1974, and all over the world. What was different, other than sheer professional-

ford and made by MGM.

These might have been good entertainment; they were certainly vintage Margaret Rutherford; but in Nima's view they had little to do with her beloved Miss Marple. *Orient Express*, however, she recognised was different; a galaxy of talent gathered together and playing Agatha Christie straight, with loving attention to character and period and absolute faithfulness to the plot. At least the last film Nima saw of her work was in all probability the best.

Other films followed, none of that startling quality of *Orient Express*, but still more than quietly successful before the company set up to manage Nima's copyrights a few years before, of which I was by now Chairman, felt strong enough to tackle television. This was a monster Nima had never tackled herself largely because she strongly disapproved of the vast majority of television as an instrument of force and influence in modern society. She felt it distracted people (particularly young people) from reading and tended to distort issues beyond recognition. You could never convince Nima that television by its portrayal of scenes of violence did not itself contribute to what she saw as the increasingly violent and selfish society which she saw developing during the last years of her life. She did not own a television until late in life and she and Max only then watched the news and current affairs programmes. She was emphatically not fascinated by it as a medium. However, under the expert guidance of Brian Stone, Ed Cork's successor as her agent, we have harnessed considerable talents to exploit television as a means of conveying the mystery and fascination of Agatha Christie to an audience large numbers of whom, it must be remembered, have never been inside a bookshop. We started with *Why Didn't They Ask Evans* adapted by a great fan called Pat Sandys and directed by Tony Wharmby. Numerous productions followed by both ITV and BBC, sometimes masterminded by Michael Grade, wherever he happened to be working. But to have made use of the various talents of Guy Slater, Trevor Bowen, etc. culminating in the incomparable performance of Joan Hickson as Miss Marple has surely enriched the evenings of television watchers all over the world. If I have one regret, it is that Nima never saw Joan Hickson as Miss Marple, lovingly

Portrait of Agatha Christie by Oskar Kokoschka.

Tony Martin

home in Wales is Nima's portrait by Oskar Kokoschka the famous expressionist painter. It is a strong picture, full of bold brush strokes and greens and blues. Nima was, I think, fascinated by the idea of being painted and fascinated by Kokoschka himself. After he had got over his initial disappointment that Nima refused to drink whisky with him at the sittings (she was actually a complete teetotaller not from any kind of moral conviction or belief, but simply from taste) he loved her too. After a hard mornings work, they both repaired to Boodle's, my club in London, where Kokoschka ate Kippers and drank Irish

ism? Perhaps for the first time Agatha Christie was associated with almost a cult film. To certain people in the entertainment business, she became fashionable again.

Nima saw this film right at the end of her life. It has to be said that she was always nervous of, almost suspicious of, the film medium. This was perhaps because she recognised it was very different from writing, and also because she could not control the finished article. Thus she thought disasters might occur, and indeed nearly did in the 1960's with some very imaginative stories based on Miss Marple starring Margaret Ruther-

Agatha with two llamas, on a visit to Paignton Zoo.

"dressed up" in her shawl, with her piercing blue eyes, a touch of asperity or impatience with stupid inspectors but real understanding and patience with young people. It was a memorable performance and perhaps almost sufficient to restore Nima's confidence in the medium.

So we have reached the evening of Nima's life. She grew old very gracefully, working as much as she could and lavishing a great deal of attention on her dog Bingo, who adored her and defended her vigorously by biting most visitors to Wallingford. Gradually, however, she got weaker, and finally on a cold January day in 1976 she died. Inevitably I suppose her funeral was a media event (how that would have horrified Nima) with cameras peering everywhere, but the Memorial Service a few weeks later was a magnificent affair glittering with publishing and entertainment personalities at St Martins in the Field, Trafalgar Square. For everybody there, Agatha Christie and her work had made an indelible impression. For her family, we could remember a loyal, loving supporter of everything we did. For us, the memories will remain as long as the books. They will be more personal, but greatly cherished.

MATHEW PRICHARD

The Queen Of Crime On The Radio

The crime serial production was something of a pioneer effort by the BBC: J. R. Ackerley of the Corporation's Talks Departments had commissioned Dorothy L. Sayers to create a six-part serial, *Behind The Screen*, in which six famous crime writers were invited to write an episode apiece and read it on the air. Dorothy and Agatha were the only women to take part, the other contributors being Hugh Walpole, Anthony Berkeley, E. C. Bentley and Ronald Knox. A novel feature of this serial was that listeners were invited to contribute solutions to the mystery to *The Listener* magazine before the finale!

Though Agatha later confessed to suffering a little from stage fright while reading her episode – the second, in which she introduced several false clues – she enjoyed the experience enough to agree to a second appearance the following year in a longer, twelve episode story, *The Scoop*, about a journalist killed while investigating a murder. She wrote the second and fourth episodes in conjunction with Dorothy L. Sayers, Anthony Berkeley, E. C. Bentley and two other distinguished crime novelists, Clemence Dane and Freeman Wills Croft.

Because of her novel writing commitments and the tight schedule of the serial, Agatha actually broadcast her contributions to *The Scoop* from a BBC relay station not far from her home in Devon and consequently felt more at ease than she had done in London. She was not, however, prepared to work on a third serial when approached once again by J. R. Ackerley. "The energy to devise a series is much better employed in writing a couple of books," she told the man from the BBC firmly but politely. "So there it is! With apologies."

Though this was to be Agatha's last personal appearance on the radio, the appeal of her work to listeners had been demonstrated beyond any doubt and ever since that time her books have been

Radio has the distinction of being the only entertainment medium on which Agatha Christie herself appeared. Twice, in the 1930s, Agatha took part in crime serials devised by that other famous detective novelist, Dorothy L. Sayers, and was heard reading her own work by those who possessed radio sets.

Although Agatha's voice was described by the producer of the first of these serials as "a little on the feeble side – but quite adequate", it did mark the beginning of an association with broadcasting that continued throughout the intervening sixty years.

© BBC

catching the imagination of generation after generation of radio producers. Indeed, there are those both inside and outside radio broadcasting who believe her work has been most effectively and evocatively produced over the air waves. There is only space here to mention just a few of the highlights of Agatha Christie on radio.

In 1947 Agatha was invited by the BBC to write a special half-hour play as part of the celebrations marking the 80th birthday of Queen Mary. The Queen Mother had been asked to select an evening of her favourite programmes and as an avid Christie reader – like most of the members of the Royal Family – had especially asked for one of Agatha's thrillers. What the authoress produced for that evening of May 26 was to become the basis of arguably her most famous creation.

Agatha had, in fact, been mulling over an idea for a while which she felt fitted the bill and quickly wrote *Three Blind Mice* which the radio maestro, Martyn C. Webster, produced with an excellent cast including Barry Morse, Gladys Young and Raf de la Torre. Shortly afterwards, Agatha re-wrote the play as a novella and then – in 1952 – turned it into a three act thriller, the most enduring play on the London stage, *The Mousetrap* . . .

In 1947, the BBC initiated what has since become almost an annual event, the *Christie for Christmas* when on December 27 they broadcast an adaptation of *Ten Little Niggers* featuring Denys Blakelock, Howard Marion-Crawford and Gladys Young. When this remarkable story was two years later adapted for television, it became the first of Agatha's works to have been used in all the four mediums of entertainment — on the stage, in films, radio and TV.

Early the following year Agatha contributed one of the best-remembered half-hour plays to the long-running series, *Mystery Playhouse* — a grisly tale of murder, *Butter in a Lordly Dish* in which a notorious womaniser is dispatched by a nail driven into his forehead. Martyn C. Webster was again the producer and Richard Williams and Lydia Sherwood the stars.

Five years later, in 1953, the BBC produced the first dramatised serial based on one of Agatha's books. Curiously, the choice was neither a Poirot or Miss Marple story, but a series of 13 adventures of the resourceful young detective partnership of Tommy and Tuppence Beresford. The two central characters were played by Richard Attenborough and Sheila Sim — an astute piece of casting as the couple were then playing to full houses in London in *The Mousetrap*!

Agatha wrote one more 30-minute play especially for radio in 1960 called *Personal Call* about the mysterious death of a woman under the wheels of a train which starred Ivan Brandt, Barbara Lott and Vivienne Chatterton. The critic of *The Listener* in praising the production declared that "the Detective Story, against all probability, seems to be coming back to radio."

For Agatha, as is self evident, it had never really gone away. And the tradition has continued to this day with a number of excellent productions of Hercule Poirot stories – featuring Peter Sallis and John Moffatt – not to mention a fine adaptation of *The Sittaford Mystery* with Geoffrey Whitehead as the quietly persistent Inspector Narracott. Only Miss Marple has yet to make her radio debut – surely a case for investigation by the BBC?   PETER HAINING

Queen Mary, the Queen Mother, at whose request Agatha wrote the radio play "Three Blind Mice" in 1947.

Paris: Agatha Christie, in the dock on the set of "Witness For The Prosecution".

"Why Not Write A Play?"

Not surprisingly, almost all of her plays are murder mysteries, about half of which are original works for the stage, while the other half are adaptations by Agatha Christie of her crime novels. The only full-length play which is not a murder mystery, is *Akhnaton*, which reflects the playwright's interest in archaeology. Set in ancient Egypt in the reign of the Pharaoh Akhnaton, it deals with the Pharaoh's attempt to persuade a polytheistic Egypt to turn to the worship of one deity, Aton, the Sun god.

Although Agatha Christie was at the height of her fame as a crime novelist when she wrote *Akhnaton* in 1937, she failed to get her play produced, perhaps because its plot commented on the folly of attempting to appease an aggressor. This was not a popular stance to adopt in 1937.

Agatha Christie's earliest play, *Black Coffee*, is one of her most fascinating, for it features her most popular detective, Hercule Poirot, in a murder mystery

The fact that one of Agatha Christie's plays, *The Mousetrap*, has broken all theatrical records, opening in London in 1952 and giving no indication, so far, that it will ever close, has tended to obscure the fact that Dame Agatha wrote sixteen other plays, some of which enjoyed highly successful runs, and most of which are still frequently performed by amateur theatre groups all over the world as well as occasionally being revived professionally.

which, since it has never been turned into a novel, is barely known to the huge army of Agatha Christie's readers.

It may well have been because she was dissatisfied with *Alibi*, a 1928 stage adaptation by Michael Morton of her Poirot novel, *The Murder of Roger Ackroyd*, in which Charles Laughton played the Belgian sleuth, that Mrs Christie decided two years later to try her hand at putting Poirot on the stage in an original play.

In 1939, one of the most ingeniously plotted of all the Christie novels appeared. This was *Ten Little Niggers*, a title which at that time gave little or no offence in Great Britain, but was changed to *And Then There Were None* for its American publication. Ten people on an island are murdered, one by one. When only two are left, there are still surprises to come. It must have been extraordinarily difficult to find a way of putting this plot on the stage, but Agatha Christie was determined to tackle it. When her play opened at the St. James's Theatre in London in November, 1943, the critic of the *Daily Telegraph* wrote: "She must play fair because her reputation depends on it. She must stick to her pattern. And she must somehow contrive to keep you and me guessing, even when the choice of suspects has narrowed down. Well, she succeeds."

In 1938, when *Appointment with Death*, an Hercule Poirot mystery set in Jerusalem and Petra, was published, Agatha Christie confessed to an interviewer that there were moments when she felt "Why – why – why did I ever invent this detestable, bombastic, tiresome little creature?" Seven years later, when she turned *Appointment with Death* into a play, she made a number of significant changes, chief among them being the deletion of Poirot from the cast of characters. In fact, in all four of the Poirot novels which she was to adapt for the stage, Agatha Christie removed her great detective from the proceedings.

She had seen Poirot portrayed on the stage in adaptations of her novels by other dramatists, and she had begun her own playwriting career with *Black Coffee* in which Poirot was the leading character. By 1945, the year in which she adapted both *Appointment with Death* and another Poirot mystery, *Death on the Nile*, for the stage, she appears to have come to the conclusion that Poirot simply did not work in the theatre, perhaps because he was too overwhelming a personality and thus tended to dwarf the other characters. Another unusual aspect of *Appointment with Death* is that the character who, in the novel, had turned out to be the murderer, is perfectly innocent in the play. More than this it would not be proper to reveal.

In its transfer to the stage, *Death on the Nile* underwent a slight change of title to *Murder on the Nile*. Gone were not only Poirot but also several of the novel's choicest suspects. Other characters had their names and their personalities altered, and there is a significant difference between the endings of novel and play. Six years later Agatha Christie turned her novel *The Hollow* into a play. In her view, the novel had been ruined by having Poirot in it. "He did his stuff all right, but how much better, I kept thinking, would the book have been without him. So when I came to write the play, out went Poirot."

Percy Marmont who played the judge in the original production of Agatha Christie's "Witness For The Prosecution" at the Winter Garden Theatre in 1953.

W ith the success of *The Hollow* as a play in 1951, Agatha Christie's golden period in the theatre began. In the next three years she was to go on to even greater heights. "I find", she said during this period, "that writing plays is much more fun than writing books. For one thing you need not worry about those long descriptions of places and people. And you must write quickly if only to keep the mood while it lasts, and to keep the dialogue flowing naturally."

The Mousetrap, which Agatha Christie adapted from her short story, *Three Blind Mice*, is discussed elsewhere in this publication. The play which followed it, *Witness for the Prosecution*, an absorbing courtroom drama with an astonishing twist in its tail, is also an adaptation of a story, one with the same title. The author

herself thought this the best play she had written, and audiences obviously concurred, for it clocked up 468 performances in London in 1953-54 and achieved an even longer run of 646 performances in New York, with the New York Drama Critics' Circle choosing it as the Best Foreign Play of the year. (The award for best American play that year went to Tennessee Williams' *Cat on a Hot Tin Roof*.)

It was for the popular British film star, Margaret Lockwood who, tired of her *femme fatale* roles in films, wanted to do a modern comedy on stage, that Agatha Christie wrote her next play, a completely original light-hearted comedy thriller which did not attempt to rival the complex plots of her other plays. It provided Margaret Lockwood with a delightful role as the wife of a diplomat who finds she has to dispose of an unexpected corpse in the library before her husband brings an important foreign politician home to dinner. *Spider's Web* arrived in the West End in December, 1954, and stayed for 774 performances, joining *The Mousetrap* and *Witness for the Prosecution*. Agatha Christie now enjoyed the rare distinction of having three plays running simultaneously in London.

In 1956 the author, in collaboration with Gerald Verner, turned her 1944 novel, *Towards Zero*, into a play. Set in the West Country of England which she knew so well, this is one of the most attractive and most mystifying of her crime novels, and the play offers an additional thrill just before its final curtain, for which there is no precedent in the novel.

Verdict, two years later, was an original play which had a disappoin-

Margaret Lockwood, appearing in the "Spider's Web" at the time, attends the first night of another Christie play "Towards Zero" with the author.

tingly brief run in London. But Agatha Christie thought it her best play after *Witness for the Prosecution*. "It failed, I think", she wrote in her autobiography, "because it was *not* a detective story or a thriller. It *was* a play that concerned murder, but its real background and point was that an idealist is always dangerous, a possible destroyer of those who love him." *Verdict* was booed on its first night, not because the audience felt cheated at not having been offered a mystery to be solved, but because the assistant stage manager rang the curtain down on the final scene about forty seconds too soon. This prevented the surprise re-entrance of an important character, and completely changed the ending of the play! Agatha Christie also felt that her original title *No Fields of Amaranth* would have been better than *Verdict*.

Undeterred by the failure of *Verdict*, Agatha Christie wrote another completely new play very quickly. *The Unexpected Guest* opened in London in August, 1958, only some weeks after *Verdict* had closed, and it ran for a very satisfactory eighteen months. With its murder victim mischievously based on the author's own brother, *The Unexpected Guest* is one of the best of her plays, its dialogue taut and effective, and its plot full of surprises despite being economical and not over-complex. It demonstrates, incidentally, the profound truth that seeing is not believing.

Then in her late sixties, Agatha Christie was to go on producing her crime novels for a good fifteen years. But her next play was to prove disappointing. This was *Go Back for Murder*, which she adapted in 1960 from her Hercule Poirot novel, *Five Little Pigs*, of seventeen years earlier. The novel, in addition to being a first-rate murder mystery, was more complex in structure than the majority of Poirot's cases, containing much vivid yet subtle characterization. The murder victim, a famous painter, is no romanticised artist-figure but a real and convincing personality, some of whose less attractive traits suggest that they might have been borrowed from Augustus John.

As had become customary, Poirot was banished from the stage version. A personable young solicitor takes his place, helping to solve the mystery and unmask the murderer. The thoroughness with which Agatha Christie completely refashioned her material for the stage

George Roubicek, Patricia Jessel and Gerard Heinz in Agatha Christie's "Verdict" at the Strand Theatre. 1958.

was impressive, but the play limps badly, and its flashback scenes are unsatisfactory. It closed after 31 performances, and has rarely been revived.

Two years after the failure of *Go Back for Murder*, the author returned to the West End with three one-act plays, produced under the collective title of *Rule of Three*. Tension is well sustained in *The Rats*, a tautly effective little melodrama involving only four characters, one of whom is described by the author as "a young man of twenty-eight or -nine, the pansy type, very elegant and amusing, inclined to be spiteful." The other characters are more charitably described, but they are all rats of a kind,

Christopher Sandford, Winifred Oughton, Violet Farebrother, Nigel Stock, Philip Newman, Renee Asherson, and Paul Curran in "The Unexpected Guest" by Agatha Christie at the Duchess Theatre.

though only two find themselves caught in a trap.

The central play, *Afternoon at the Seaside*, is rather disappointing, though it provides a certain light relief from the more dramatic atmosphere of the other two. There is a wisp of a plot concerning a stolen necklace, but the real charm of the play lies in its curiously old-fashioned, pre-war picture of the lower-middle classes relaxing on a crowded beach. Uneconomically, it calls for a cast of twelve. The final play, *The Patient*, is set in a private room in a nursing-home where ingenious means are found to enable a woman, totally paralyzed and unable to speak after a fall from her balcony, to indicate whether she fell accidentally or was pushed.

Rule of Three received mixed reviews, and survived for no more than ten weeks. These three plays proved to be Agatha Christie's farewell to her London theatre public, for her final play, which she wrote ten years later when she was over eighty, closed without reaching the West End. This was *Fiddlers Three* which was first toured in 1971 as *Fiddlers Five*. Revised and given a new title, it re-opened in Guildford the following year, toured quite successfully for several weeks, but failed to find a London theatre. *Fiddlers Three* combines comedy and crime in a somewhat inconsequential manner. Its dialogue is light rather than witty, and to succeed in the theatre today it would need performers of extraordinary insouciance and charm.

During Agatha Christie's lifetime, four plays adapted by others from her novels or stories were produced, to be followed by two more after her death in 1976. These were *Alibi*, adapted by Michael Morton in 1928 from *The Murder of Roger Ackroyd*, which starred Charles Laughton as Poirot; *Love from a Stranger*, adapted by Frank Vosper in 1936 from a short story, "Philomel Cottage"; *Peril at End House*, adapted by Arnold Ridley in 1940, with Francis L. Sullivan as Poirot; and *Murder at the Vicarage*, adapted by Moie Charles and Barbara Toy in 1949, with Barbara Mullen as Miss Marple. The posthumous adaptations, both the work of Leslie Darbon, were *A Murder is Announced*, with Dulcie Gray as Miss Marple in 1977; and *Cards on the Table* in 1981 which took a leaf from Agatha Christie's script, so to speak, and eliminated Poirot from the cast.

CHARLES OSBORNE

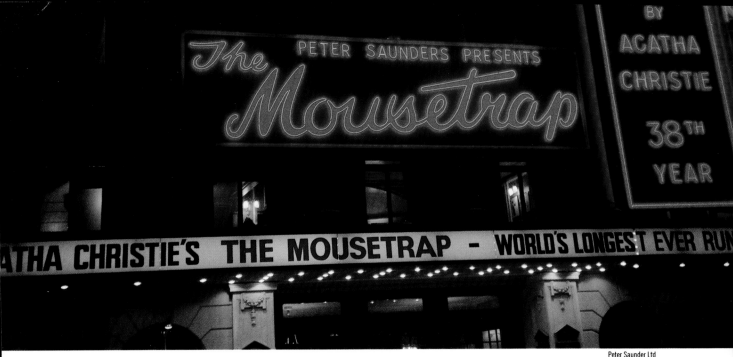

"You Made Theatrical History Tonight"

Sir Peter Saunders.

Those words were spoken to Agatha Christie on the occasion of the tenth anniversary of her play *The Mousetrap* by Peter Saunders, the play's producer. Since then the play has reached its 38th year on the West End stage and is the longest running play anywhere in the world.

The story behind this phenomenon is really about two people's uncanny ability to tap the popular fancy of the theatre-going public – Agatha Christie and Peter Saunders.

Agatha Christie had an extraordinary instinct for the stage and what mattered" says Sir Peter Saunders in his elegant office near the Savoy Hotel. Ask him what accounts for the extraordinary success of *The Mousetrap* and he puts it down to two essential ingredients – Agatha Christie's flair for writing a superb story and his

own belief in unceasing promotion. "An Agatha Christie play has, if you like, all the components of a really good panel game – comedy, drama, puzzles – people can bring the family and sit back and enjoy it."

To quote from one of Sir Peter's many press releases about the show "Since the Mousetrap opened on 25th November 1952, it has been seen by more than 8 million people; 236 actors and

actresses have appeared in the play; there have been 111 understudies; 68 miles of shirts have been ironed; over 271 tons of ice cream and approximately 52,000 gallons of squash and minerals have been consumed by patrons. The play has been presented in 44 different countries and translated into 24 languages."

It all started quite modestly really. In 1947 the BBC wanted to do a special

Allan McClelland, Richard Attenborough and Aubrey Dexter in the original 1952 production of "The Mousetrap".

radio broadcast to celebrate Queen Mary's birthday. They approached Her Majesty and asked her what she would like, expecting a concert perhaps, opera or Shakespeare. Queen Mary promptly replied "An Agatha Christie play" and so the authoress duly obliged with a thirty minute radio play called "Three Blind Mice".

Meanwhile, a struggling impresario called Peter Saunders had written to Agatha Christie's agent, Edmund Cork and asked if he could be considered when Cork was next looking for a producer for a Christie play. Up until then all the West End productions of her plays had been handled by Bertie Meyer but, as luck would have it, Meyer was offered "The Hollow" but was unable to cast it and abandoned it. Cork offered it to Saunders. It was a success – the number one Christie fan, Queen Mary, came to a matinee at the Fortune Theatre – and the result was that Agatha invited Peter to spend the weekend at her house in Devon, Greenway. It was the start of a tremendous friendship. Peter Saunders, always the great enthusiast, was the perfect business partner for the shy and sometimes uncertain Agatha. Some months later she presented him with a script – "Three Blind Mice", rewritten into a full-length play. The

name was changed to *The Mousetrap* and the rest, as they say, is history.

Agatha was to say later about Peter Saunders "He is one of my most appreciated friends; he has influenced me in many ways. I have enjoyed his friendship and his good company – his ready humour, the knowledge of the stage he has imparted to me, and I have a deep respect for the things he has made me do that I said I couldn't and didn't want to do . . .

His kindness to me over my shy fits – my terror and misery at first nights – was most soothing and also over my invariable belief that a play would not run . . . he assured me that *The Mousetrap* would run at least a year or longer. Dear Peter – he was always the most consoling person, and he was certainly right that time."

The play opened at the Ambassadors Theatre on 25th November 1952 with the popular star Richard Attenborough in the lead role. His wife Sheila Sim was also in the cast. The public flocked to the box office.

"There was a hungry theatre-going public after the war" explains Sir Peter "and limited forms of other entertainment. For example, on the day *The Mousetrap* opened, the TV column of *The Times* was just 3$\frac{1}{2}$ lines long!"

After 18 months, film commitments forced Richard Attenborough to leave the play and it would have been catastrophic for the box office were it not for the fact that the Peter Saunders publicity machine swung into operation.

Peter had developed his talents for PR long before he became an impresario. A long spell as a newspaper journalist in Glasgow had taught him the value of a good news story and a period as Publicity Agent for the Harry Roy Band taught him how to create news stories almost out of thin air.

Each anniversary of the play was celebrated with a mammoth party to which stars of the stage and screen, even royalty, were invited. The press loved them.

Weddings, births and even divorces amongst the cast were reported. Cartoons appeared in the dailies; on the thousandth performance every member of the audience received a free silk programme; the millionth visitor to the show found the press waiting and Sir Peter loaded down with presents for her. Soon, *The Mousetrap* became a legend.

"Publicity seems to be self-perpetuating" reflects Sir Peter "Anything and everything that occurred during the day-to-day running of the play was seized upon and offered to the press." Within recent years, for the 36th anniversary, Sir Peter gathered together thirty actresses who had been leading ladies over the years in the play and this remarkable picture was featured in the World Press and television.

At a massive party for the tenth year of the run, Agatha Christie made one of her rare appearances and even rarer speeches. She said "I do feel an enormous debt of gratitude to all the casts, the actors and actresses who have played in *The Mousetrap* and they have made it such a success. They have all been good casts and have all brought something to it of their own. It is wonderful to have known so many actors and actresses and to find what a charming lot of people they are and how warm-hearted and kindly."

Sir Peter says that at this stage he had no idea that *The Mousetrap* was in for at least another twenty years run and certainly not that he would now be planning to take the play to its 40th year

A scene from the 1989/90 production of "The Mousetrap".

in 1992.

During his career he has produced a total of 11 original Agatha Christie plays in the West End (amongst other things of course) and such is his belief in her ability to draw the crowds that it has always been her name that he features large and bold above the title of the play. He always involved Agatha in casting and auditions because he trusted her judgement and vision implicity.

Now, in his own words, he is "winding-down", but *The Mousetrap* still occupies a lot of his time, He still supervises the unceasing production of publicity, he writes each year's commemorative brochure and he picks the new director and new cast for the show every August. He personally goes through the CV's and photos of 3-400 actors and actresses, then auditions and short-lists over a period of three weeks.

"One of the secrets of the play is that it is beautifully constructed" he says "so when I interview directors I look for the ones who say that they don't really want to change it. It's like a good Dundee cake really, you may change the cook but don't muck about with the recipe or you'll spoil it."   LYNN UNDERWOOD

ST. MARTIN'S THEATRE   WEST STREET CAMBRIDGE CIRCUS WC2

Evenings at 8·00   Tuesday at 2·45
Saturday at 5·00 & 8·00

PETER SAUNDERS presents

THE MOUSETRAP

AGATHA CHRISTIE by

38th YEAR

WORLD'S LONGEST EVER RUN!

LIAM KENNEDY
CHARLES STAPLEY
BRIAN SPINK
SOPHIE DOHERTY
JONATHAN DRYSDALE
PENELOPE FREEMAN
RICHARD CROXFORD
and
KATHLEEN BYRON

Date	1928
Title	ALIBI
Source Material	*The Murder of Roger Ackroyd* Book published 1926
Author	Adapted by Michael Morton
Premiere	May 15th, 1928 at Prince of Wales' Theatre, London
Director	Gerald du Maurier
Cast	Lady Beerbohm Tree, Charles Laughton, Jane Welsh, Henry Daniell, Basil Loder, Iris Noel, Henry Forbes Robertson, Gillian Lind, J.H. Roberts, Cyril Nash, Norman V. Norman, John Darwin, J. Smith Wright, Constance Anderson.

Date	1930
Title	BLACK COFFEE
Source Material	None – original work
Author	Agatha Christie
Premiere	December 8, 1930 at the Embassy Theatre, London
Director	Andre Van Gyseghem
Cast	Francis L. Sullivan, Donald Wolfit, Josephine Middleton, Joyce Bland, Lawrence Hardman, Judith Mentrath, Andre Van Gyseghem, Wallace Evennett, John Boxer, Richard Fisher, Walter Tennyson, Frank Follows, George F. Wiggins.

Date	1936
Title	LOVE FROM A STRANGER
Source Material	Short story *Philomel Cottage* published 1934
Author	Adapted by Frank Vosper
Premiere	March 31, 1936 at the New Theatre, London
Director	Murray MacDonald
Cast	Muriel Aked, Norah Howard, Marie Ney, Frank Vosper, Geoffrey King, Charles Hodges, Esma Cannon, S. Major Jones.

Date	1937
Title	AKHNATON
Source Material	None, original work
Author	Agatha Christie This play was published in 1973 in volume form but has only been produced in rep.

Date	1940
Title	PERIL AT END HOUSE
Source Material	Book *Peril At End House* published in 1932
Author	Adapted by Arnold Ridley
Premiere	May 1, 1940 at the Vaudeville Theatre, London
Director	A.R. Whitmore
Cast	Wilfred Fletcher, Donald Bisset, Tully Comber, Phoebe Kershaw, Francis L. Sullivan, Ian Fleming, Olga Edwardes, William Senior, Beckett Bould, Josephine Middleton, Isabel Dean, Brian Oulton, May Hallatt, Charles Mortimer, Margery Caldicott, Nancy Poultney.

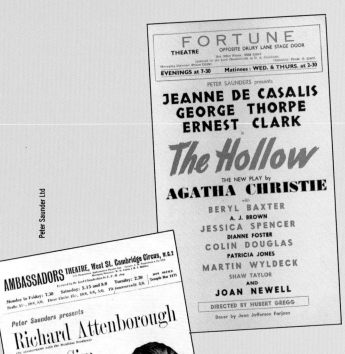

Peter Saunder Ltd

Agatha Christie Plays

Date	**1943**
Title	TEN LITTLE NIGGERS (later retitled AND THEN THERE WERE NONE)
Source Material	Book *Ten Little Niggers* published in 1939
Author	Agatha Christie
Premiere	November 17, 1943 at the St. James' Theatre, London
Director	Irene Hentschel
Cast	William Murray, Hilda Bruce-Potter, Reginald Barlow, Linden Travers, Terence de Marney, Michael Blake, Percy Walsh, Eric Cowley, Henrietta Watson, Allan Jeayes, Gwyn Nicholls.

Date	**1945**
Title	APPOINTMENT WITH DEATH
Source Material	Book *Appointment with Death* published in 1938
Author	Agatha Christie
Premiere	March 31, 1945 at the Piccadilly Theatre, London
Director	Terence de Marney
Cast	Mary Clare, Deryn Kerbey, Ian Lubbock, Beryl Machin, John Glennon, Percy Walsh, Anthony Dorset, Janet Burnell, Joan Hickson, Gerard Hinze, Carla Lehmann, Alan Sedgwick, John Wynn, Harold Berens, Owen Reynolds, Cherry Herbert, Corinne Whitehouse, Joseph Blanchard.

Date	**1946**
Title	MURDER ON THE NILE (opened as HIDDEN HORIZON on 9 April 1945 in Wimbledon)
Source Material	Book *Death On The Nile* published in 1937
Author	Agatha Christie
Premiere	March 19, 1946 at the Ambassadors Theatre, London
Director	Claude Guerney
Cast	Richard Spranger, Christmas Grose, James Roberts, Helen Hayes, Joanna Derrill, Ronald Millar, Jacqueline Robert, Hugo Schuster, Ivan Brandt, Rosemary Scott, David Horne, Vivienne Bennett, Walter Lindsay.

Date	**1949**
Title	MURDER AT THE VICARAGE
Source Material	Book *Murder At The Vicarage* published in 1930
Author	Adapted by Moie Charles and Barbara Toy
Premiere	December 16, 1949 at the Playhouse, London
Director	Reginald Tate
Cast	Jack Lambert, Genine Graham, Michael Newell, Betty Sinclair, Michael Derbyshire, Andrea Lea, Barbara Mullen, Mildred Cottell, Alvys Maben, Reginald Tate, Francis Roberts, Stanley Van Beers.

Date	**1951**
Title	THE HOLLOW
Source Material	Book *The Hollow* published in 1946
Author	Agatha Christie
Premiere	June 7, 1951 at the Fortune Theatre, London
Director	Hubert Gregg
Cast	Beryl Baxter, George Thorpe, Jeanne de Casalis, Jessica Spencer, A.J. Brown, Colin Douglas, Patricia Jones, Joan Newell, Ernest Clark, Dianne Foster, Martin Wyldeck, Shaw Taylor.

Date	**1952**
Title	THE MOUSETRAP
Source Material	Radio Play *Three Blind Mice* broadcast in 1947
Author	Agatha Christie
Premiere	November 25, 1952 at the Ambassadors Theatre, London
Director	Hubert Gregg
Cast	Sheila Sim, John Paul, Allan McClelland, Mignon O'Doherty, Aubrey Dexter, Jessica Spencer, Martin Miller, Richard Attenborough.

Date	**1953**
Title	WITNESS FOR THE PROSECUTION
Source Material	Short Story *The Witness For The Prosecution* published 1933 in *The Hound of Death*
Author	Agatha Christie
Premiere	October 28, 1953 at the Winter Garden Theatre, London
Director	Wallace Douglas
Cast	Rosalie Westwater, Walter Horsbrugh, Milton Rosmer, Derek Blomfield, David Horne, David Raven, Kenn Kennedy, Patricia Jessel, Philip Holles, Percy Marmont, D.A. Clarke-Smith, Nicolas Tannar, John Bryning, Denzil Ellis, Muir Little, George Dudley, Jack Bulloch, Lionel Gadsden, John Farries Moss, Richard Coke, Agnes Fraser, Lauderdale Beckett, Iris Fraser Foss, David Homewood, Graham Stuart, Jean Stuart, Peter Franklin, Rosemary Wallace.

Date	**1954**
Title	SPIDERS WEB
Source Material	None, original work
Author	Agatha Christie
Premiere	December 13, 1954 at the Savoy Theatre, London
Director	Wallace Douglas
Cast	Felix Aylmer, Harold Scott, Myles Eason, Margaret Lockwood, Margaret Barton, Judith Furse, Sidney Monckton, Charles Morgan, John Warwick, Campbell Singer, Desmond Llewelyn.

Date	**1956**
Title	TOWARDS ZERO
Source Material	Book *Towards Zero* published in 1944
Author	Adapted by Gerard Verner
Premiere	September 4, 1956 at the St James' Theatre, London
Director	Murray MacDonald
Cast	Cyril Raymond, Mary Law, Gillian Lind, Frederick Leister, George Baker, Janet Barrow, Gwen Cherrell, Michael Scott, William Kendall, Max Brimmell, Michael Nightingale.

Date	**1958**
Title	VERDICT
Source Material	None, original work
Author	Agatha Christie
Premiere	May 22, 1958 at the Strand Theatre, London
Director	Charles Hickman
Cast	George Roubicek, Gretchen Franklin, Patricia Jessel, Gerard Heinz, Derek Oldham, Viola Keats, Moira Redmond, Norman Claridge, Michael Golden, Gerald Sim.

Peter Saunders Ltd

We gratefully acknowledge the assistance of Sir Peter Saunders in providing the material for this article.

Date	**1958**
Title	THE UNEXPECTED GUEST
Source Material	None, original work
Author	Agatha Christie
Premiere	August 12, 1958 at the Duchess Theatre, London
Director	Hubert Gregg
Cast	Philip Newman, Renee Asherson, Nigel Stock, Winifred Oughton, Christopher Sandford, Violet Farebrother, Paul Curran, Michael Golden, Tenniel Evans, Roy Purcell.

Date	**1960**
Title	GO BACK FOR MURDER
Source Material	Book *Five Little Pigs* published in 1943
Author	Agatha Christie
Premiere	March 23, 1960 at the Duchess Theatre, London
Director	Hubert Gregg
Cast	Robert Urquhart, Peter Hutton, Ann Firbank, Mark Eden, Anthony Marlowe, Laurence Hardy, Lisa Daniely, Margot Boyd, Dorothy Bromiley, Nigel Green.

Date	**1962**
Title	RULE OF THREE (*Three One Act Plays*)
Source Material	None, original work
Author	Agatha Christie
Premiere	December 20, 1962 at the Duchess Theatre, London
Director	Hubert Gregg
Cast	Betty McDowall, Mercy Haystead, David Langton, Raymond Bowers, Michael Beint, Robert Raglan, Mabelle George, Vera Cook, John Quayle, John Abineri, Margot Boyd, Robin May, Rosemary Martin.

Date	**1972**
Title	FIDDLERS THREE
Source Material	Original play called *Fiddlers Five* which was reworked by the author
Author	Agatha Christie
Premiere	1st August, 1972, Yvonne Arnaud Theatre, Guildford, Surrey
Director	Allan Davis
Cast	Doris Hare, Raymond Francis, Arthur Howard

Date	**1977**
Title	A MURDER IS ANNOUNCED
Source Material	Book *A Murder Is Announced* published in 1950
Author	Adapted by Leslie Darbon
Premiere	September 21, 1977 at the Vaudeville Theatre, London
Director	Robert Chetwyn
Cast	Patricia Brake, Dinah Sheridan, Eleanor Summerfield, Christopher Scoular, Mia Nadasi, Dulcie Gray, Barbara Flynn, Nancy Nevinson, Michael Dyerball, James Grout, Michael Fleming, Gareth Armstrong.

Date	**1981**
Title	CARDS ON THE TABLE
Source Material	Book *Cards on the Table* published in 1936
Author	Adapted by Leslie Darbon
Premiere	December 9, 1981 at the Vaudeville Theatre, London
Director	Peter Dews
Cast	Lynette Edwards, William Eedle, Margaret Courtenay, Belinda Carroll, Pauline Jameson, Derek Waring, Gary Raymond, Gordon Jackson, Charles Wallace, James Harvey, Patricia Driscoll, Mary Tamm, Jeanne Mockford, Henry Knowles.

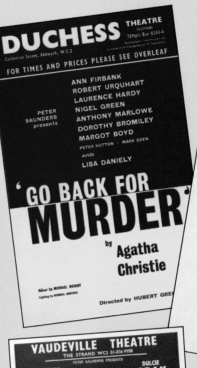

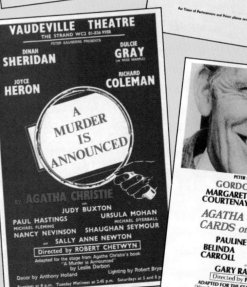

Peter Saunders Ltd

Murder And Mystery

It remains a curious fact that the first of Agatha's characters to be brought to the screen was neither Hercule Poirot nor Miss Marple, but the enigmatic Mr. Harley Quin, 'The Love Detective' who made his debut in a magazine story, *The Coming of Mr. Quin* written in the late 1920s. Adapted for the screen by Leslie Hiscott, the story of Mr. Quin and his almost supernatural ability to come to the aid of persecuted lovers, was retitled *The Passing of Mr. Quinn* (with no explanation as to why the extra 'n' was added to his name) and starred one of the matinee idols of the Twenties, Stewart Rome.

Initially, it was hoped to make this film the first of a series, but a luke-warm reception at the box office caused the producer, Julius Hagen of Strand Films, to turn his attention to perhaps where it should have been right from the start: Hercule Poirot. In 1931, Hagen filmed *The Murder of Roger Ackroyd* adapted from the earlier stage play, *Alibi* (1928) in which Charles Laughton had been the star in both the British and American productions. Yet to play Poirot, the producer cast another tall, dark matinee idol, Austin Trevor, who was physically and temperamentally the complete opposite of the character in the books!

Despite these discrepancies, *The Murder of Roger Ackroyd* was a success in the British cinema – the general public did not then have the set notions about Poirot they do today – and Hagen filmed two other stories, *Black Coffee* (based on the play of that name) in 1931 and *Lord Edgware Dies* in 1934. Austin Trevor, though, always remembered these pictures rather ruefully because of the liberties taken with the Belgian detective.

Somewhat earlier than this series – indeed only a few months after the release of *The Passing of Mr. Quinn* – a German film-maker, Fred Sauer, brought Tommy and Tuppence Beresford to the screen in a rather loose adaptation of *The Secret Adversary* (1929). Playing the two leading characters as kind of Jazz Age flappers were the blonde English actress, Eva Gray, and the Italian stunt-man-turned-actor, Carlo Aldini.

Ann Harding, Basil Rathbone and Donald Calthrop in the film, "Love From A Stranger", 1937.

From the days of the silent movies to today's wide-screen extravaganzas, the crime and mystery stories of Agatha Christie have proved a constant attraction for film makers in Britain, America and once even in Europe. But despite the fact that over two dozen films have been made from her books, only a handful have done justice to her work and most of those which she saw during her lifetime, "gave me too many heartaches" to quote her own words. Author Peter Haining takes a look at some of these films and their stars.

Basil Rathbone, one of the leading screen actors of the Thirties, made a sinister central character in the adaptation of Agatha's short story about a terrorised young wife, *Philomel Cottage*, which had first been made into a play, *Love From A Stranger*, in 1936, and then filmed the following year. An enjoyable and at times exciting movie, it is also notable for a fine piece of character playing in the role of the maid Emmy by a young actress named Joan Hickson (known to television viewers of the 1980's as the 'definitive' Miss Marple). *Love From A Stranger* was later remade in Hollywood in 1947, though much less satisfactorily, with John Hodiak and Sylvia Sidney.

The year 1945 saw the release of the first – and still one of the very few – classic screen versions of an Agatha Christie story: 20th Century-Fox's *And Then There Were None* based on the 1939 novel, *Ten Little Niggers*. Brilliantly and innovatively directed by the Frenchman, Rene Clair, and packed with experienced actors such as Barry Fitzgerald, Walter Huston, Louis Hayward and C. Aubrey Smith, the picture was acclaimed by public and critics alike. Since this

On The Silver Screen

From the film, "And Then There Were None", 1945.

Charles Laughton in "Witness For The Prosecution".

Margaret Rutherford and Thorley Walters in the film, "Murder She Said".

version, the story has been filmed again three times – including one version especially for television – but all have failed to equal the excellence of the original.

The beautiful English actress Margaret Lockwood initially relished her role in *Spider's Web* which she filmed for the Danziger brothers in 1956. Not the least of her reasons for optimism was the fact that Agatha herself had prepared the screenplay based on her own stage version launched two years earlier. The picture was also the first Christie story to be made in colour. Sadly, though, after a number of delays, when the picture was finally released in 1960 the high hopes of everyone connected with it were dashed by poor reviews and even poorer box office returns.

The year 1957, however, saw the release of the second undisputed classic Christie movie – Billy Wilder's masterful screen interpretation of the authoress' courtroom drama, *Witness for the Prosecution*. Time and money was lavished on the filming of this intriguing mystery by United Artists and the leading roles were all played by highly skilled actors: including Charles Laughton as Sir Wilfred Roberts; Tyrone Power as Leonard Vole the man on trial for his life; and Marlene Dietrich as his desperate wife. The resultant picture was an undoubted *tour de force* and well deserves the regular reshowings it is given on television. The picture only narrowly missed winning the six Oscars for which it was nominated.,

It was the turn of Miss Marple to make her bow in the cinema next – in the portly and formidable form of Margaret Rutherford in a series produced by MGM between 1962 and 1964. Such was the stamp that Margaret put on the role that she created a public image of the lady detective from St. Mary Mead which has persisted in a great many people's minds until the recent superb new interpretation by Joan Hickson.

Though Margaret Rutherford was undeniably a popular Miss Marple she

Louis Hayward, June Duprez, Richard Haydn, Judith Anderson and Sir C. Aubrey Smith in the film, "Ten Little Niggers".

Elke Sommer, Alberto de Mendoza, Oliver Reed and Maria Rohm in the film, "And Then There Were None".

later admitted to having been reluctant to take on the role in the first place because of her distaste of violence in any shape or form. Yet once cast – with her real-life husband Stringer Davis, as her assistant, Mr. Stringer – she gave splendidly over-the-top performances under the direction of George Pollack in a total of four pictures: *Murder She Said* (1962), *Murder at the Gallop* (1963), *Murder Most Foul* (1964) and *Murder Ahoy* (1964). A curious footnote to these pictures is that the second and third pictures were actually based on novels which had originally featured Hercule Poirot! And the fourth film was not even based on an Agatha Christie story.

In 1966, MGM switched their attention to Hercule Poirot and filmed *The Alphabet Murders* – based on the 1936 novel, *The ABC Murders* – with another apparently unlikely actor cast as the Belgian detective: the American comedy star, Tony Randall. Nor did the director Frank Tashlin seem any better suited to the task for his previous pictures had included Jerry Lewis comedies and Bugs Bunny cartoons! Yet it has to be said that Randall used effective make up and gave a restrained performance and made a much better Poirot than expected, though Robert Morley succeeded in turning Captain Hastings into a rather bumbling, Watson-like assistant.

Then in 1974 came *Murder On The Orient Express*, filmed by producers John Brabourne and Richard Goodwin for EMI, which heralded a whole new era of Christie on film. The script, by Paul Dehn was faithful to the original story, beautifully staged and directed by Sidney Lumet, and Poirot was painstakingly played by its star, Albert Finney. Almost hidden beneath face packs and bolstered around the middle by padding, the youthful Finney created a wholly believable Poirot and was given excellent support by his co-stars John Gielgud, Sean Connery, Lauren Bacall, Wendy Hillier, Jaqueline Bisset, Jean-Pierre Cassel, Vanessa Redgrave, Rachel Roberts, Richard Widmark, Michael York, Colin Blakely, George Colouris, Dennis Quilley, Ingrid Bergman and Anthony Perkins. The picture deservedly won three British Film Awards and six Oscar nominations.

When a second Poirot movie, *Death on the Nile* was made by EMI in 1978, Finney decided against playing the detective again and into his shoes stepped that actor-of-many-parts, Peter

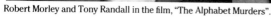

Robert Morley and Tony Randall in the film, "The Alphabet Murders".

From the film, "Murder On The Orient Express".

AGATHA CHRISTIE'S
DEATH ON THE NILE

A murderer strikes on board the luxury Nile steamer *Karnak* – and Hercule Poirot faces his most baffling case.

NAT COHEN presents for EMI

a JOHN BRABOURNE / RICHARD GOODWIN production   a JOHN GUILLERMIN film

PETER USTINOV

JANE BIRKIN · LOIS CHILES · BETTE DAVIS · MIA FARROW · JON FINCH · OLIVIA HUSSEY · I.S. JOHAR
GEORGE KENNEDY · ANGELA LANSBURY · SIMON MacCORKINDALE
DAVID NIVEN · MAGGIE SMITH · JACK WARDEN

AGATHA CHRISTIE'S DEATH ON THE NILE

Music by NINO ROTA · Screenplay by ANTHONY SHAFFER · Produced by JOHN BRABOURNE and RICHARD GOODWIN · Directed by JOHN GUILLERMIN · Technicolor ® · Distributed by EMI Films Limited

EMI

From the film, "Ordeal By Innocence".

From the film, "Appointment With Death".

Ustinov, to offer a new but equally engrossing interpretation. With a script by Anthony Shaffer and picturesque location shooting along the Nile – not to mention some fine playing by Bette Davis, David Niven and Maggie Smith – the picture reinforced the belief that if Agatha's stories were adhered to by the film-makers the results could be both critically and publicly acclaimed. Angela Lansbury's performance in this film led to her being asked to play Miss Marple in *The Mirror Crack'd*.

Peter Ustinov has since played Poirot twice more for the cinema in *Evil Under the Sun* (1981) and *Appointment with Death* (1987) and three times for television in *Thirteen at Dinner* (1985), *Dead Man's Folly* (1986) and *Murder in Three Acts* (1986). Of these performances, *Evil Under The Sun* ranks perhaps the best after *Death on the Nile* with Ustinov again supported by some fine acting by Colin Blakely, Maggie Smith, James Mason and Diana Rigg.

From the film, "The Mirror Cracked".

EVIL IS EVERYWHERE. EVEN IN PARADISE.

AGATHA CHRISTIE'S
EVIL UNDER THE SUN

EMI

In 1980, EMI decided to give Miss Marple the same lavish treatment with Angela Lansbury in the title role for their production of *The Mirror Crack'd*. Unfortunately, the tragedy of the assassination of Lord Mountbatten on his boat in Ireland in which his son-in-law and the film's producer, John Brabourne, was injured, seriously affected the making of this picture. Angela Lansbury's part was somewhat restricted as other parts were expanded to suit a number of big name American stars including Elizabeth Taylor, Tony Curtis, Rock Hudson and Geraldine Chaplin – but she has subsequently gone on to earn international acclaim playing a writer-turned-sleuth, Jessica Fletcher, in a TV series called *Murder She Wrote* in which she stars as a kind of cross between Miss Marple and Agatha Christie herself!

One of Agatha's favourite novels, *Ordeal By Innocence* (1958), was filmed by the Cannon Group in 1985 with a typically absorbing performance by Donald Sutherland as the inquisitive physician, Dr. Arthur Calgary. Filmed on the author's native Devon coast, the picture also co-starred Faye Dunaway, Ian McShane, Sarah Miles and Christopher Plummer.

The Christie archives are today, of course, still full of riches for film-makers, though the control over which books are to be filmed and how they will be made are rigorously and wisely controlled by Agatha Christie Ltd (of which Agatha's daughter and grandson are directors) as a direct result of the various failures during the past sixty years. Among those stories which have been tentatively earmarked for movies are the Sergeant Battle investigation, *Towards Zero* (1944) and Agatha's only mystery story with a historical setting, *Death Comes as the End*, which is set against the Egypt she explored with her archaeologist husband.

The most jealously guarded film rights of all are, perhaps not surprisingly, those for *The Mousetrap*. Though here a special stipulation which Agatha herself insisted upon many years ago still holds good – no film is to appear until at least six months after the end of the stage run. And who would be brave enough to predict just when *that* might be!

The full details of "The Mirror Crack'd" are revealed for the first time in Peter Haining's new book Murder in Four Acts *published by W. H. Allen.*

PETER HAINING

TRAFALGAR FILMS present

a **MAX SCHACH** production

Ann **HARDING**

WITH *Basil* **RATHBONE**

in

LOVE FROM A STRANGER

From the play by FRANK VOSPER
Based on a short story by AGATHA CHRISTIE
Screenplay and Dialogue by FRANCES MARION

with

BINNIE HALE

Directed by
ROWLAND V. LEE

ASSOCIATE PRODUCER
HARRY E. EDINGTON

Released thru UNITED ARTISTS

The Complete List Of

Date	1928
Title	DIE ABENTEUER G.m.b.H. ADVENTURE INC.)
Source Material	Book *The Secret Adversary* published 1922
Director	Fred Sauer
Stars (Silent film)	Carlo Aldini, Eve Gray, Michael Rasumny

Date	1928
Title	THE PASSING OF MR. QUIN
Source Material	Short Story *The Coming of Mr. Quin*
Director	Leslie Hiscott
Stars (Silent film)	Trilby Clark, Ursula Jeans, Stewart Rome

Date	1931
Title	ALIBI
Source Material	The Play *Alibi*, Dramatisation by Michael Morton of *Murder of Roger Ackroyd*
Director	Leslie Hiscott
Stars	Austin Trevor (Poirot), Elizabeth Allen, Clare Greet, Franklin Dyall

Date	1931
Title	BLACK COFFEE
Source Material	Play *Black Coffee* premiered 1930
Director	Leslie Hiscott
Stars	Austin Trevor (Poirot), Adrienne Allen, Richard Cooper (Hastings), Melville Cooper (Japp), C. V. France

Date	1934
Title	LORD EDGWARE DIES
Source Material	Book *Lord Edgware Dies* published 1933
Director	Henry Edwards
Stars	Austin Trevor, Jane Carr, Richard Cooper, John Turnbull

Date	1937
Title	LOVE FROM A STRANGER
Source Material	Play of the same name from the Short Story *Philomel Cottage* published 1934
Director	Rowland V. Lee
Stars	Ann Harding, Basil Rathbone, Binnie Hale, Bruce Seton, Jean Cadell, Brian Powley, Joan Hickson, Donald Calthrop, Eugene Leahy

Date	1945
Title	AND THEN THERE WERE NONE
Source Material	Book *Ten Little Niggers* published 1939
Director	Rene Clair
Stars	Barry Fitzgerald, Walter Huston, Louis Hayward, Roland Young, June Duprez, C. Aubrey Smith, Judith Anderson, Mischa Auer, Richard Haydn, Queenie Leonard

Agatha Christie Films

Date	**1947**
Title	LOVE FROM A STRANGER
Source Material	1937 film of the same name, play of the same name, Short story *Philomel Cottage*
Director	Richard Whorf
Stars	John Hodiak, Sylvia Sydney, Ann Richards, John Howard, Isobel Elsom, Ernest Cossart, Anita Sharp-Bolster, Philip Tonge, Fred Warlock
Date	**1957**
Title	WITNESS FOR THE PROSECUTION
Source Material	Play of the same name, Short story of the same name published 1933
Director	Billy Wilder
Stars	Tyrone Power, Marlene Dietrich, Charles Laughton, Elsa Lanchester, John Williams, Henry Daniell, Ian Wolfe, Una O'Connor, Torin Thatcher, Frances Compton, Norma Varden, Philip Tonge, Ruta Lee, Molly Roden, Otiola Nesmith, Marjorie Eaton
Date	**1960**
Title	SPIDER'S WEB
Source Material	Play of the same name premiered in 1954
Director	Godfrey Grayson
Stars	Glynis Johns, John Justin, Jack Hulbert, Cicely Courtneidge
Date	**1962**
Title	MURDER SHE SAID
Source Material	Book *4.50 From Paddington* – U.S. *What Mrs McGillicuddy Saw* published 1957
Director	George Pollock
Stars	Margaret Rutherford, Arthur Kennedy, Muriel Pavlow, James Robertson Justice, Charles Tingwell, Ronald Howard, Thorley Walters, Conrad Phillips, Joan Hickson, Ronnie Raymond, Stringer Davis, Gerald Cross, Michael Golden
Date	**1963**
Title	MURDER AT THE GALLOP
Source Material	Book *After the Funeral* published 1953
Director	George Pollock
Stars	Margaret Rutherford, Robert Morley, Flora Robson, Charles Tingwell, Stringer Davis, Duncan Lamont, Katya Douglas, James Villiers, Robert Urquhart, Gordon Harris
Date	**1964**
Title	MURDER MOST FOUL
Source Material	Book *Mrs. McGinty's Dead* published 1952
Director	George Pollock
Stars	Margaret Rutherford, Ron Moody, Charles Tingwell, Megs Jenkins, Ralph Michael, Andrew Cruikshank, James Bolam, Stringer Davis, Francesca Annis, Allison Seebohm, Dennis Price, Terry Scott

Once in 50 years

YOU'LL TALK ABOUT IT!

suspense like this!

—BUT PLEASE DON'T TELL THE ENDING!

EDWARD SMALL PRESENTS

TYRONE POWER
MARLENE DIETRICH
CHARLES LAUGHTON

WITNESS FOR THE PROSECUTION

ARTHUR HORNBLOW'S PRODUCTION
OF AGATHA CHRISTIE'S SUSPENSE MASTERPIECE

with ELSA LANCHESTER
JOHN WILLIAMS

TORIN THATCHER
UNA O'CONNOR
PHILLIP TONGE
IAN WOLFE

From the story and stage play by
AGATHA CHRISTIE

Screenplay by
BILLY WILDER & HARRY KURNITZ

Adaptation by
LARRY MARCUS

Directed by
BILLY WILDER

Produced by
ARTHUR HORNBLOW · RELEASED THRU UA UNITED ARTISTS

The Kobal Collection

Date	**1964**
Title	MURDER AHOY!
Source Material	Not a Christie story but a story by David Pursall and Jack Seddon
Director	George Pollock
Stars	Margaret Rutherford, Lionel Jeffries, Charles Tingwell, Stringer Davis, William Mervyn, Francis Matthews, Terence Edmund, Tony Quinn, Joan Benham, Gerald Cross, Derek Nimmo, Norma Foster, Roy Holder, Bernard Adams, Henry Longhurst, Henry Oscar, Miles Malleson

Date	**1965**
Title	TEN LITTLE INDIANS
Source Material	Play *Ten Little Niggers* from novel of same
Director	name published 1939
Stars	George Pollock
	Hugh O'Brian, Shirley Eaton, Fabian, Leo Genn, Stanley Holloway, Marianne Hoppe, Wilfrid Hyde White, Dahlia Lavi, Dennis Price, Mario Adorf

Date	**1966**
Title	THE ALPHABET MURDERS
Source Material	Book *The ABC Murders* published 1936
Director	Frank Tashlin
Stars	Tony Randall, Anita Ekberg, Robert Morley, Maurice Denham, Guy Rolfe, Sheila Allen, James Villiers, Julian Glover, Grazina Frame, Clive Morton, Cyril Luckham

Date	**1972**
Title	ENDLESS NIGHT
Source Material	Book *Endless Night* published 1967
Director	Sidney Gilliat
Stars	Hayley Mills, Hywel Bennett, Britt Ekland, Per Oscarsson, George Sanders

Date	**1974**
Title	MURDER ON THE ORIENT EXPRESS
Source Material	Book *Murder On The Orient Express* published 1934
Director	Sidney Lumet
Stars	Albert Finney, Lauren Bacall, Martin Balsam, Ingrid Bergman, Jacqueline Bisset, Jean Pierre Cassel, Sean Connery, John Gielgud, Wendy Hiller, Anthony Perkins, Vanessa Redgrave, Rachel Roberts, Richard Widmark, Michael York, Colin Blakely, George Colouris, Dennis Quilley

Date	**1975**
Title	TEN LITTLE INDIANS
Source Material	Play *Ten Little Niggers* published 1939
Director	Peter Collinson
Stars	Oliver Reed, Elke Sommer, Stephanie Audran, Charles Aznavour, Richard Attenborough, Gert Frobe, Herbert Lom, Maria Rohm, Adolfo Celi, Alberto de Mendoza

Date	**1978**
Title	DEATH ON THE NILE
Source Material	Book *Death On The Nile* published 1937
Director	John Guillermin
Stars	Peter Ustinov, Mia Farrow, Lois Chiles, Simon MacCorkindale, Bette Davis, Maggie Smith, David Niven, Angela Lansbury, Olivia Hussey, Jack Warden, George Kennedy, Sam Wannamaker, Jane Birkin, Jon Finch
Date	**1980**
Title	THE MIRROR CRACK'D
Source Material	Book *The Mirror Crack'd From Side to Side* published 1962
Director	Guy Hamilton
Stars	Angela Lansbury, Geraldine Chaplin, Tony Curtis, Edward Fox, Rock Hudson, Kim Novak, Elizabeth Taylor, Marella Oppenheim, Wendy Morgan, Margaret Courtenay, Charles Gray, Maureen Bennett, Carolyn Pickles, Eric Dodson, Charles Lloyd Pack
Date	**1982**
Title	EVIL UNDER THE SUN
Source Material	Book *Evil Under The Sun* published 1941
Director	Guy Hamilton
Stars	Peter Ustinov, Colin Blakely, Jane Birkin, Nicholas Clay, Maggie Smith, Roddy McDowell, Sylvia Miles, James Mason, Dennis Quilley, Diana Rigg, Emily Horne, John Alearson, Paul Antrim, Cyril Conway
Date	**1985**
Title	ORDEAL BY INNOCENCE
Source Material	Book *Ordeal By Innocence* published 1958
Director	Desmond Davis
Stars	Donald Sutherland, Christopher Plummer, Faye Dunaway, Sarah Miles, Ian McShane, Billy McColl
Date	**1988**
Title	APPOINTMENT WITH DEATH
Source Material	Book of the same name published 1938
Director	Michael Winner
Stars	Peter Ustinov, Lauren Bacall, Carrie Fisher, John Geilgud, Hayley Mills, Piper Laurie, Jenny Seagrove
Date	**1989**
Title	TEN LITTLE INDIANS
Source Material	American Publication *Ten Little Indians* 1939
Director	Alan Birkinshaw
Stars	Donald Pleasance, Herbert Lom, Frank Stallone, Sarah Maur Thorp

The small screen makes Christie magic

Joan Hickson as Miss Marple.   © BBC

Television which has recently produced a number of widely acclaimed series of Agatha Christie stories – in particular those featuring Hercule Poirot and Miss Marple – in fact gave her work a most inauspicious start when the BBC produced the first TV play of *Ten Little Niggers* in 1949.

Admittedly in the immediate post war years, the BBC Television Service was still in its infancy – not to mention still recovering from the enforced austerity of World War II when the screens had been blank for six years – but those among the less than a million viewers in Southern England who possessed the tiny 12-inch black and white sets saw a production of Agatha's classic story of multiple murder set on a small island off the Devon coast which varied from the acceptable to the laughable.

The 90 minute version of the stage

Agatha Christie did not, herself, possess a television until very late in life. In fact, she positively disapproved of the medium as she felt it had an adverse affect on the quality of life.

However, after her death, it was felt by her family and fellow trustees of the Agatha Christie company that television would be the only way to reach new audiences and persuade a new generation to read the Christie books. It has proved hugely successful, not just in the UK but all over the world.

Peter Haining charts the development of Agatha Christie on television, from its shaky beginnings to its present level of excellence.

play was directed by Kevin Sheldon and transmitted live – as were most programmes on TV then – starring John Bentley (of Paul Temple fame), Arthur Wontner (a former film Sherlock Holmes), Margery Bryce, Bruce Belfrage, Elizabeth Maude and Campbell Singer. Shown on a Saturday evening as one of the highlights of the week, the adaptation was unfortunately beset by most of the problems experienced by the embryo service: occasionally out-of-focus pictures, a piece of scenery falling at a dramatic moment, the sound boom swinging into view, and as the *piece de resistence*, one of the actors who had just been stabbed standing up in full view of the camera and strolling off the set with his hands in his pockets!

It was perhaps just as well that Agatha Christie in her West Country home could not see this transmission – though she certainly heard all about it from others who *did* – for it would have done nothing to change her distrust of the medium. This attitude persisted throughout her life and it is only to be regretted that she did not live to see the recent triumphs by both the BBC and Independent Television Companies.

Coincidentally, her work also made its debut on American television in 1949, where programmes were also live, in black and white, though technically perhaps a little more sophisticated. The first production was a Halloween night adaptation of *Witness For The Prosecution* based not on the famous play (which, of course, Agatha did not write until 1953), but on the original short story in her collection, *The Hound of Death & Other Stories* (1933). The play was for the weekly series, Chevrolet Tele-Theater, and the central role of the lawyer, Mr. Mayherne, who takes on the case of Leonard Vole accused of misappropriating an old woman's money, was played by E.G. Marshall, a young actor destined eventually for fame as another lawyer, Lawrence Preston, in the long-running TV series, *The Defenders*.

The play was clearly a success, for twice in the next three years it was repeated on other series. The first time in November 1950 on the live drama show, *Danger*, starring John Donovan, and directed by a man destined for bigger things in front of the cameras in Hollywood, Yul Brynner. The third production, on the Lux Video Theater in September 1953, was perhaps the most notable of the versions because starring

as the attorney was a famous film star best known for playing gangster roles, Edward G. Robinson.

American TV continued to enjoy something of a love affair with Agatha's stories in the Fifties – and can also claim to have launched Poirot, Miss Marple and the detective partnership of Tommy and Tuppence Beresford on the small screen. In August 1950, the weekly drama series The Web – produced by Mark Goodson and Bill Todman of game show fame – adapted *Three Blind Mice* from the 1947 BBC radio play, and starred Richard Kiley, Henry Hull and Mary Sinclair. That same year in November, Fireside Theater presented a 30-minute version of *The Golden Ball*, starring George Nader and Eve Miller, taken from Agatha's 1934 collection, *The Listerdale Mystery*. This production has the distinction of being the first of her stories to have been pre-filmed for TV – thereby making it a more polished and less accident prone transmission than any of its predecessors.

A week before Christmas 1950, the Nash Airflyte Theater achieved a landmark by first introducing two of the authoress' series characters to viewers – presenting Tommy and Tuppence in a

remarkably faithful version of *"The Case of the Missing Lady"* from *Partners in Crime* (1929). The two young sleuths were played by the handsome leading man, Lee Bowman, and Barbara Bel Geddes, nowadays Miss Ellie in the top TV series, *Dallas*.

In 1952, the top rated US series, *Suspense*, produced an eerie version of another story from *The Hound of Death*, *"The Red Signal"*, featuring Tom Drake as the man receiving supernatural warnings.

Miss Marple made her television debut in the US on December 30, 1956 in an hour-long adaptation of *"A Murder Is Announced"* on the Goodyear Playhouse. Not only was this a first for the lady detective from St. Mary Mead, but also the first of Agatha Christie's stories to be shown on TV in colour. A former British musical hall star turned actress, Gracie Fields, was a perhaps unlikely Miss Marple, and there was also a small role for another English actor destined one day to play James Bond, the sauve Roger Moore.

To complete the introduction of the trio of Agatha Christie's most famous characters, Poirot made his first appearance on the small screen in April

David Suchet as Hercule Poirot and Pauline Moran as Miss Lemon.

1962 in a half-hour General Electric Theater presentation entitled *Hercule Poirot*, but which was actually an adaptation of the short story, *"The Disappearance of Mr. Davenheim"*, in which the little Belgian solves a mystery without leaving his apartment. Playing the detective was a well-known character actor, Martin Gabel, and the story was introduced by the General Electric Theater host, one Ronald Reagan! The teleplay was intended to be the pilot for a series, but despite such luminaries the audience rating was not big enough to justify more episodes.

Jeanne Moreau in the Granada ITV network drama, Agatha Christie's "The Last Seance".

Obviously, Agatha Christie saw none of these American presentations, and those which were made of her work in Britain only compounded her general disappointment with television adaptations – which is one of the main reasons why so few of her stories were made available for the medium during her lifetime. Indeed, it has only been since her death, and in particular during the last decade during which television has had access to the most sophisticated filming techniques, ideal location shooting and substantial budgets usually underwritten by other overseas television companies, that justice has really been done to her excellent characters and ingenious plots.

London Weekend Television can take a lot of the credit for starting this new era of Christie on Television with their bold decision to make an authentic, star-studded version of *Why Didn't They Ask Evans?* in 1980. Inspired, no doubt, by EMI's success with their faithful adaptation of *Murder on the Orient Express* for the cinema and the films that followed, LWT producers Tony Wharmby and Jack Williams, cast Francesca Annis and James Warwick as two young sleuths trying to solve the mystery of a man found dying near a golf course, and co-starred John Gielgud, Eric Porter, Bernard Miles, Connie Booth and Madeline Smith.

The enthusiastic press and public reaction encouraged LWT to follow this the next year with *The Seven Dials Mystery*, the death-by-poisoning case investigated by two bright young things – with James Warwick as the male lead again and Cheryl Campbell as an effervescent Lady Eileen 'Bundle' Brent. Again

Anthony Higgins and Norma West in Granada's drama, Agatha Christie's "The Last Seance".

Michael Aldridge as Dr. Lavington in "The Mystery Of The Blue Jar".

Osmund Bullock and Sarah Berger in "The Girl In The Train".

John Gielgud was in the cast with Harry Andrews, Terence Alexander, Rula Lenska and Leslie Sands.

Once more the reception for this production encouraged LWT to invest £2 million in a Christie series, their choice falling on the adventures of Tommy and Tuppence, as they hoped to repeat the success of earlier male/female crime partnerships on TV such as Patrick Macnee and Honor Blackman in The Avengers and Robert Wagner and Stefanie Powers in Hart to Hart. Producer Jack Williams did not have far to look for casting his principals – picking the successful pairing of James Warwick and

An overhead view of the creation of a scene for "The Agatha Christie Hour" for the television series.

Partners in Crime, James Warwick and Francesca Annis in "Affair Of The Pink Pearl".

Partners in Crime, James Warwick and Francesca Annis in "The Sunningdale Mystery".

Francesca Annis from *Why Didn't They Ask Evans?* to be Tommy and Tuppence.

A two hour version of the novel *The Secret Adversary* opened the series in October 1983, and was then followed by nine one hour long adventures under the generic title, *Partners in Crime*. James Warwick's performance as Tommy has one newspaper calling him "a new kind of sex symbol", while Francesca Annis, as always, was a delight to viewers' eyes.

The year before this, 1982, Thames Television also launched a new Christie series which was the first to cull stories from a number of her collections and it was screened as The Agatha Christie Hour. Pat Sandys who had scripted LWT's two earlier murder mysteries was the producer of the series and created ten dramas, two of which "The Case of the Middle Aged Man" and "The Case of the Discontented Soldier" featured Maurice Denham as another of the authoress' series characters, the investigator Parker Pyne. This latter story also had Lally Bowers playing Ariadne Oliver, Agatha's light-hearted version of herself!

At Christmas that same year, the BBC made another rather more successful attempt at bringing a Christie play to the screen, selecting the old Margaret Lockwood stage play success, *Spider's Web*, and casting Penelope Keith – "TV's favourite bossy boots" to quote a Daily Express critic – as Clarissa Hailsham-Brown, the upper class lady who discovers a body in her living room. The production, with co-stars, Robert Fleming, Thorley Walters and Elisabeth Spriggs, provided ideal escapist Christmas entertainment according to press and viewers alike.

One success then lead to a triumph for the BBC when, in 1984, with a masterful piece of casting, they launched the first of their Miss Marple series, *The Body in the Library*, with Joan Hickson as the ideal lady detective. Nine further adaptations have confirmed Joan as the definitive Miss Marple and the series as one of the best ever seen on television. (Two competing American TV adaptations of *A Caribbean Mystery*, 1983, and *Murder With Mirrors*, 1985, starring Helen Hayes as Miss Marple have really not been the equal, despite the star's venerable performances.)

In the interim – starting in 1989 – LWT with the superlative actor David Suchet have created a similarly authentic and much praised series of *Poirot* cases. At the time of writing the company have transmitted two series of adventures under the general title, *Agatha Christie's Poirot*. Which Suchet most certainly *is!*

There have been two other recent television productions which also deserve mention here. Granada TV's 1986 version of *"The Last Seance"* included in their series Shades of Darkness, and highlighted by a mesmerising performance by the great French actress, Jeanne Moreau, as the spiritualist medium, Madame Exe. And the same year, TVS producer Nick Evans had the clever idea of devising a confrontation between Agatha Christie and Poirot, the detective who came to "hang round my neck like the old man of the sea", to quote his creator, in an hour-long play, *Murder By The Book*. Ian Holm made an excellent Poirot and Dame Peggy Ashcroft a formidable Agatha Christie.

The idea of the meeting was that only one of the two people should survive. But what the story actually proved – as have all the recent adaptations of Christie on TV – is that both the creator's fame and the appeal of her characters to audiences everywhere show every sign of remaining just as potent for years to come...

PETER HAINING

A Tribute To Agatha

It is over 50 years since I first met Agatha shortly after the publication of *The Murder Of Roger Ackroyd* had made her famous. The blurb of her new detective novel gave away a vital clue, and my uncle sent me, young and innocent, to break the terrible news. I was received with the greatest kindness, but little did I think at the time that this was the beginning of a long and very special personal friendship with one of the most wonderful and modest people I have ever met.

By her bedside, Agatha kept her mother's copy of *The Imitation of Christ* by Thomas A. Kempis, and on the fly leaf under her name Agatha Mallowan, she had written: *"Who shall separate us from the love of Christ?*

Shall tribulation, or distress, or persecution or famine, or nakedness, or pen, or sword. . .?

I am persuaded that neither death, nor life, nor angels, nor principalities, nor powers, nor things present, nor things to come, not height nor depth, nor any other creature, shall be able to separate us from the love of God, which is in Christ Jesus our Lord."

That loving and lovely passage thoughtfully extracted from a chapter in St. Paul's Epistle to the Romans was her last message and is a reflection of the gentle Christian spirit that resided within her.

It is in this way perhaps that she would wish to be remembered, in spite of her world-wide fame as an author whose legacy to us is something over 85 books, one for each year of her life. Incomparable master, so we may call her, of detective fiction, she has held spellbound a multitude of readers the world over and to her embarrassment wherever she travelled, Agatha was likely to be hailed as a living wonder, for there was never any one more genuinely modest. Her philosophy is aptly ex-

When Agatha Christie died in 1976, after a life of writing almost unequalled by any other author, it was fitting that the valedictory address at her memorial service should be given by Sir William Collins, of the Collins publishing empire — Agatha's publishers for the greater part of her life. We reproduce it here because it gives an intimate insight into the spirit of the lady who was, without a doubt, the world's most appreciated author.

pressed by a quotation which one evening towards the end of her life she selected for a boy of 11 at his request. It ran:

"I have three treasures,
Guard them and keep them safe.
The first is love,
The second is never do too much,
The third is never be the first in the world,
Through love one has no fear.
Through not doing too much one has amplitude of reserve power.
Through not presuming to be the first in the world one can develop one's talent and let it mature."

To the end of her days she was totally unspoiled by her fame as a novelist and playwright, whose films also sometimes enjoyed an incomparable success in the cinema. In the world of the theatre where she made so many friends, she will be remembered as a household name and as a great entertainer who was never morbid and enjoyed the longest known continuous run on the London stage, *"The Mousetrap"*.

In her own genre of literary work we must accord her the title of genius although she herself would never have admitted to any deep-seated literary pretensions. But she possessed in supreme measure one mark of literary

greatness, the art of telling a story and holding a reader in its thrall, mesmerised by the narrative. Her characters often lightly but always subtly sketched are alive when we overhear their conversation as we enter into the room, seated or standing with them. Agatha had an extraordinary faculty of picking up bits of conversation and throwing them into a dramatic and sometimes tortuous plot which usually defied the reader's ability to unravel and convincingly arrived at its unexpected and brilliant end, whether guided by the cynical realism of Hercule Poirot or by the quiet and unobtrusive subtlety of that acutely observant old lady Miss Marple, never without a touch of humour.

The exciting signposts guided the narrative but deep down there was a strong and underlying sense of purpose. Agatha herself liked to think of her detective novels, not merely as preoccupied with the solution of crime, but as the equivalent of the medieval morality play, concerned with the interplay of the forces of good and evil, wherein the bad man was always brought to book, often with a flourish of trumpets. We find that this problem of good and evil is never far absent for instance in *Endless Night*, one of her own favourites. She had a gift also

Godfrey Argent

for apt and sometimes recondite quotation and showed an easy familiarity with the Scriptures as in the apocalyptic title of The Pale Horse, whose rider's name was Death, and Hades followed him.

One and all who had the good fortune to know her or to be familiar with her work could not but admire the versatility of her talent which was combined with a gusto for life. She savoured the delights of travel and no one has given us a more lively picture of life in the Orient, which she shared with her husband in the field of oriental archaeology, so happily described in *Come, Tell Me How You Live*, full of humour and comic incidents. On the other hand her penetrating understanding of psychology and her admiration of courage, which she deemed one of the highest virtues, were best illustrated in her psychological novels written under the name of Mary Westmacott, in which she had more time to probe deeply into character than in the brilliant sketches which had to suffice in suffering and supreme renunciation come out best in her novel with the poetic title, *The Rose And The Yew Tree*.

One of her books beloved by many, was *Star Over Bethlehem*, a kind of Christmas Carol with a sweet story about the little donkey watching over the birth of Christ in the manger, humorous, proud, cocky and loving.

And that is the note on which we may end – her gentle loving care for the good in man, and in beasts, for she had a succession of beloved dogs never absent from her thoughts.

In the many hundreds of letters received since her death, those who have written from many distant parts of the globe have blended admiration in equal measure with love, for Agatha knew what true religion means. The world is better because she lived in it. What greater tribute could be paid to her gentle memory?

SIR WILLIAM COLLINS
Copyright Sir William Collins 1976

The Next Ten Years?

Photograph copied by John E. May

A centenary may be many things; a celebration, a reflection on past glories, or an intellectual assessment of worth; and hopefully the Agatha Christie centenary will be all of these. One thing it certainly is not is the end of anything. As *The Mysterious Affair at Styles* was published around 1920 it can fairly be said that the books have proved that they are timeless and by the year 2000 I am confident that they will enter the twenty-first century as fresh and lively as they are today.

But they will not do this without encouragement, assistance and good management. This means we must continue to rely on the traditional values inbred in the material and presenting them attractively to the public; avoiding gimmickry and bad taste; no Agatha Christie tee-shirts or excessive emphasis on violence on covers; print must be large enough for old people to read and paperbacks must not fall apart when pages are turned. Material for films and television should be carefully chosen and lovingly presented. And we should be mindful of the need to respect traditional outlets in the book trade and not go overboard in the direction of so-called modern methods of distribution.

Nevertheless we cannot put the clock back – the nineties new ideas will enlarge and we must adapt to them. We have already begun to market audio-cassettes read by distinguished actors; one suspects this market will expand rapidly. New markets like Russia and Eastern Europe will appear, and old ones like South America will need to be encouraged far more. There will be further far-reaching technological and organisational changes in TV and video; the combination of traditional material and modern technology could be irresistible.

Finally, let me indulge in a little fiction myself – crystal ball gazing to show how the nineties might be at least as memorable as the eighties. If anybody accuses me of wishful thinking, I plead guilty but if all that follows happened, the world of entertainment would be much richer.   MATHEW PRICHARD